IN OUR LANGUAGE

Collected Poems

LYNN SAUL

Jumping
Cholla
Press

Tucson Arizona

Copyright 2014 Lynn Saul

Cover Art: Joyce Septimus, "Table Setting" (adapted)

Library of Congress Control Number: 2014900211

ISBN: 978-1884106125

Jumping Cholla Press
Tucson AZ

jumping_cholla@cox.net

for Kevin, Erica, Aiyana, and Emerson

and for my teachers,
especially Elizabeth Evans, Robert Houston, Rolly Kent, Steve
Orlen, Richard Shelton, and Ofelia Zepeda

and for Joe,
who made me promise never to write about him
but changed his mind

also by Lynn Saul

Learning to Say "Satoraljaujhely"

Chapbooks:

Family
I am Trying to Understand
Nashim B'Midbar/Desert Women

ACKNOWLEDGMENTS

I would like to thank the editors of the magazines and anthologies where many of these poems have previously appeared:

Andrew Mountain Press, "Stained Glass"
Anklam Road Review, "The Words of the Prophet"
Black Star, "A Letter to My Sister" (published here as "Breakfast Notes") and "At a Middle Eastern Restaurant"
Bubbe Meisehs, "1932"
Cache Review, "After the Accident," "Solo," and "L'Eglise St-Etienne"
Clarion, "A Cultural History in America," "Aunt Sarah," and "Visiting Aunt Florence"
Crossing Limits, "The Man Who Didn't Like to Talk" and "The Words of the Prophet"
Feminist Parenting, "To Lilith"
Flagstaff Festival of the Arts Arizona Anthem, "The Man Who Didn't Like to Talk"
Howling Mantra, "Van Gogh at the Carnegie Museum"
Jewish Women's Literary Annual, "What Leah Did," "A Midrash on Leah #2," "Mythology in Three Parts," and "How To Survive in the 21st Century"
Mazagine, "Planting by the Moon," "Interstices," and "When It is Warm on a September Night"
Mountain Newsreal, "Hugging You"
The MacGuffin, "Travels"
Pennsylvania Review, "Four Poems for Georgia O'Keeffe"
Persona, "Breakfast Notes"
Poetica, "Yedid Nefesh" and "Miriam the Prophet Speaks to Moses"
Poets at Large (Tucson Public Library), "The Colander"
SandScript, "Picking Peas," "Arizona Angel #1" and "Sick Little Girl"
Sarah's Daughters Sing, "1932," "A Midrash on Leah #1," "Leah tells Rachel...," and "Antonio's Night"
ShalomVeg, "Seder," "The Gardens," "Picking Peas," "Farm Report," and "Words of the Prophet"

Tucson Weekly, "In Our Language"
Which Lilith?, "To Lilith"

Contents

BEYOND HOLLYHOCKS

HOLLYHOCKS, AUGUST 1952 17
CLEAN MUD 19
GRAY 21
VISITING AUNT FLORENCE 24
OVER THE RIVER AND THROUGH THE WOODS 25
FIELD TRIP DAY 26
APRIL 18, 1955 28
OVER THE HILL 29
THE BUSINESSMEN'S LUNCH 30
BEDFORD SPRINGS 32
READING WILLIAM CARLOS WILLIAMS IN THE KITCHEN
ON FOLKSTONE DRIVE 33
A CULTURAL HISTORY IN AMERICA 34
VAN GOGH AT THE CARNEGIE MUSEUM 35
L'ETRANGER 36
THE BODY PUZZLE 37
IN WESTERN PENNSYLVANIA 38
THE CASTLE AT CEDAR LAKE 39

FAMILY

WHO I WANT FOR USHPIZIN IN MY SUKKAH, HOPING
THEY CAN EXPLAIN IT ALL 43
1932 45
RETURN 47
BREAKFAST NOTES 48

LOOKING FOR BARRACUDA	49
HUGGING YOU	51
MYTHOLOGY IN THREE PARTS	52
LETTER TO MY GREAT-GRANDMOTHER IN KALUSZ	54
AUNT SARAH	55
BIRTHDAY GIFT, MAY 22, 1977	56
THE WORDS OF THE PROPHET	58
LETTER TO MY GRANDMOTHER WHO HAS BECOME BLIND	59
INTERSTICES	60
FOR KEVIN'S TENTH BIRTHDAY	62
WHAT I'M HOPING TO FIND	63
DAYENU	64
HARMADIK GENÉRACIÓ MAGYAR	68
UNCLE IZ	71
GRANDMA EM'S PRAYERBOOK	72
THE CERAMIST	73
TANTE	75
THE CHALLAH COVER	76
TRANSYLVANIA	77
GRANDPA'S COUSIN	78
TRANSCRIBING THE NYIREGHAZA HUNGARY HOLOCAUST MEMORIAL	79
IN MY STUDY	80
MAY THIS CHILD	81
THE VISIT	83
THE OIL PAINTING	84
THE GARDENS	85

PAPRIKA	86
THE SILENCE AT NIGHT	87

NASHIM B'MIDBAR /WOMEN IN THE DESERT

THE WAY TO GO	91
IN OUR LANGUAGE	92
FROM THE DESERT	93
WHITE HORSES WEST OF ANEGAM	94
FOUR POEMS FOR GEORGIA O'KEEFFE	95
ARIZONA ANGEL	99
DESERT CHARCO	100
CORNCOBS	102
THE MAN WHO DIDN'T LIKE TO TALK	104
PERSEID LOVE POEM	106
BURNING STORIES	107
TO LILITH: CONSIDERATIONS ON WOMEN, MEN, CHILDREN, AND THINKING FOR YOURSELF	111
SONG FOR MIRIAM	113
MIRIAM THE PROPHET SPEAKS TO MOSES	115

THE BOOK OF LEAH

A MIDRASH ON LEAH, NO. 1	119
A MIDRASH ON LEAH, NO. 2	120
LEAH TELLS RACHEL SHE WANTS TO LEARN NOT TO LET JACOB MATTER	122
WHAT LEAH DID	123
MEDITATIONS ON THE JEWISH YEAR	125
COMFORT	127
EREV ROSH HASHANAH 5754, AT THE FOOT OF THE MOUNTAIN OF THE DESERT BIGHORN	129

YEDID NEFESH FOR EREV ROSH HASHANAH ON SHABBAT 132
STAINED GLASS 133
WE ARE AS A PASSING SHADOW, BUT YOU ARE ETERNAL. 134
MI SHEBEIRACH I 135
MI SHEBEIRACH II 136
LION OF JUDAH 137
SEASONS 138
SEDER 140
URCHATZ 142
ARIZONA THE ANGEL 143
GUARDING THE SABBATH 144

EVEN A SINGLE PASSION LURKING IN THE HEART HAS THE POWER TO OBSCURE REASON

FIVE DAUGHTERS OF THE GARMENT TRADE 149
WHEN IT IS WARM ON A SEPTEMBER NIGHT 151
THE ARTIST RETURNS TO HIS GARRET IN PARIS 152
PLANTING BY THE MOON 153
SOLO 155
AFTER THE ACCIDENT 156
THE HANDMADE DRESS 157
FOR WILL AREHART 158
DINNER AND A MOVIE WITH SUSAN AT THE HISTORICAL LANDMARK 159
FOREST FLOWER 160
TRAVELS 161
THAT NIGHT 163

THIN WALLS	165
BLUE WILLOW	166
THE COLOR OF THE MOON	167
WATER AND EARTH AND HEAVEN, FISH WOMAN BIRD	168
ANTONIO'S NIGHT	171
PITTSBURGH DREAM	173
TWICE NOW I HAVE THOUGHT	175
NIGHT OUT	176
FLOOD IN THE DESERT	178
FARM REPORT, JUNE 2001	179
ON LISTENING TO A MOZART *ANDANTE*	180
MORNING PRAYERS ON THE PATIO, TUCSON	181
THE COLANDER	182
TESHUVAH	183
TEFILLIN	185
NO SENSE OF HISTORY	188
CUTE LITTLE DARK BABY	189
NOTHING TO DO WITH BEING OR FEELING JEWISH	191
THE HUNGARIAN ART BOOKS	193
GUILLERMO KAHLO	196
TALAVERA	197
SNAKES	198
DECEMBER 9, 1980	200
OVER A BEER	201
L'EGLISE ST-ETIENNE	203
ALTER KACYZNE	204
THE YOUNG WOMAN CONSIDERS THE UNTHINKABLE	206

ASTHMA, JUNE 6, 2000	207
TOMATOES	208
NOVEMBER 22, 1963	209
THE LAST NIGHT	211
IN JANUARY	212
THE SICK GIRL	213
LACE CURTAINS	214
KOSZI, KOSZI	215

WAR/PEACE

AT A MIDDLE-EASTERN RESTAURANT	219
DREAD, PEACE, AFTER RADNOTI	220
HOW TO SURVIVE IN THE 21ST CENTURY	222
A NOTE ABOUT LANGUAGE	225
LYNN SAUL	227

JOYCE SEPTIMUS

IN OUR LANGUAGE

BEYOND HOLLYHOCKS

HOLLYHOCKS, AUGUST 1952

Hollyhocks crept
into the garage into
the doorway
between the wall
of cinder blocks
with sides that bulged
like buckled cardboard boxes
and the giant garage door,
massive as carved cathedral portals.
The hollyhocks crept
like roots into the crevice
that winds to center
in forbidden earth,
hollyhocks seeking
China, seeking
their origin,
seeking China where quince blossoms
open in the sun, where women sit,
their feet bound in black silk,
holding purple fans like waving blooms
of hollyhocks,
like water oozing toward dry cracks
in summer clay, like water
freezing in granite, like oil
in a damaged gear.
The hollyhocks
invaded dark, they crept
like snakes into the garage
jammed with tires,
oily ropes and rusted chains,
shovels, rakes,
a bicycle with a missing wheel.

The hollyhocks have green hands
the color of the forest
where Hansel and Gretel were lost,
the night forest where the lousewort

pokes through debris of oak leaves
and three spots of sunlight
point the way like crumbs
they dropped to trace their path,
not knowing how the wrens would eat them.
White hollyhocks
shock in the darkness
like amanita
and the crimson blossoms
are the bloody stubs of fingers
chopped from his bride
when the robber bridegroom
could not remove her rings. The hollyhocks
have stems like ropes that hang
from rafters, ropes black with axle grease,
ropes thick as Rapunzel's braids. In this unlit
        conservatory
hollyhocks explode
like witches' laughter in the cave.

CLEAN MUD

come in and play with clean mud
she summoned me from the collected silt of the gutter
to her ceramics studio
i watched her roll out clay like pie dough
trim it, shape it over
plaster molds
i watched her mix slip, pour it
into molds and out again
through a small hole
i never knew where it had gone
or how it could turn into a cup
i patted balls of cool clay in my own palms
pushed finger indentations into ashtrays
for grandpa, scratched waves
into the hair on little-girl statues

come in and play with clean mud
she was making the ten commandments for our new temple
my mother in my mind
might as well have been moses
that's what i thought
when i saw the finished product on the ark

come in and play with clean mud
i really didn't want to
in the gutter a sycamore leaf pushed
up against a fat twig
and maybe susie would come by
to play teacher
and maybe i could be all alone
and make up stories to myself

but in the clean mud my mother
made something out of nothing
but mud, and we ate from it,
prayed before it,

people said oh,
it's beautiful about it

my mother in my mind
might as well have been moses
that's what i thought

GRAY

I'm waiting for my mother to pick me up after dancing class. After-school ballet, ten or fifteen of us, all third-graders, in the school basement, practicing tours-jetés in little pink tutus.

The walls are gray concrete, waxed or finished with something that makes them shine and smell strange. The ceiling too, with light fixtures that hang down from solid white rods. The floor is concrete too, not quite dull, but worn more than the walls.

The teacher stands on a riser along the outside wall. The gray afternoon sky hides behind the metal grating over the grimy, gray windows high above the teacher.

And then we're done. The teacher lifts the needle from the phonograph and tells us she'll see us next Thursday. We don't change, we first put on our wool leggings and heavy coats over our tutus, and change from ballet shoes into socks and clunky leather oxfords.

Two of my friends walk home, but my mother told me she would come to get me since the crossing guard has already gone home. So I stand at the corner outside Lincoln School and watch the cars stop at the light, then go on. But my mother doesn't come, and it's getting dark.

The street lights are coming on. Red and yellow neon signs on the stores along Beverly Road. The street lights are a dirty yellow, almost gold. The sky isn't black, just a very dark gray. And my mother hasn't come yet.

There's no one left here that I know. Cars drive by, mostly coming from the city. Fathers coming home from work. My father doesn't work in the city, so he won't be coming this way. Anyhow, he is out of town on a business trip; that's why my mother has the car to come and pick me up. Where is she?

It's cold. Even with my leggings and coat, my bare skin feels cold. I miss the sweater, corduroy jumper, and knee socks I had on earlier. I should have gone to the girls' room and changed back after ballet. I've got them in the little red bag I'm carrying. My bare thighs feel strange next to the itchy woolen leggings. My bare arms feel strange, too. The bulky coat seems empty without two more layers between it and my skin.

Maybe my mother isn't coming. She's forgotten about me. She's busy with my little sister and baby brother. She's forgotten that she told me to wait here for her. It's starting to snow. I watch snowflakes land on my red sleeve and dissolve into the unruly wool fibers. I watch them melt on the gray sidewalk. I watch them blur the green, then yellow, then red traffic light over the intersection as it swings in the wind.

I start to cry. I know she's not coming. I suspect she doesn't love me. I imagine I'm an orphan, left forever on this cold, dark street corner. Snowflakes are landing on my cheeks and melting, and tears are sliding alongside them. I rub my face with my fuzzy mitten, but it doesn't help. I start to sob. I can feel the wetness all the way through to my hand.

A man comes up to me and asks me why I'm crying. I'm not supposed to talk to strangers. I've been told about the Lindberg baby, kidnapped and dead. But he hadn't been left on a cold, dark street corner by a forgetful mother. "I'm waiting for my mother to come and pick me up after my ballet class." I say this without interrupting my sobs. The man sits down on the bench next to me, and we don't say any more to each other.

I look up and see my mother pulling the car up next to the curb. I'm still sniffling and rubbing my eyes when she opens the door and says, "Let's go." She can't understand why I'm crying. It's not that late, she says. She's annoyed and I feel stupid, misunderstood. She thinks I'm acting like a baby. She thinks that I'm eight years old and I should know better.

I hate ballet. I hate the tinkly piano music and the need to count steps. I hate the pink tutu that makes my short, fat legs stand out. I hate the emptiness between my skin and the satin lining of my coat sleeves. I hate the shiny gray concrete walls and the metal grating on the grimy window. I hate having to stay after school and watch the gray sky and sit on a cold gray bench and feel the snowflakes melting on my face. I've never quit anything before.

The next morning, I announce to my mother, "I want to quit ballet."

VISITING AUNT FLORENCE

I'm eight, dressed in a starched white collar
for the trip through the spruce forests to Polk
State School and Hospital where you
are kept. In our 52 Pontiac we circle
buildings that squat like giants at the top of each hill.
Outside your cottage large women lie
in large cribs. Their arms twist like limp
windmills. On the swing a thin woman in lavender
tenses her pasty face in rhythm with the chains.
I know that somehow you are different. You

can't talk. My father asks you questions,
translates your answers for the rest of us.
I report on school and swimming. I panic
when you grunt and squeal your pride. My father says
we'll take you for a ride. I help to wheel you
to the car. They lift your lumpy body in.
We drive to the Isaly's in Oil City, we each
get a dime for a Klondike, and you grin
your inscrutable smile while the chocolate drips across
the collar of the dress my mother chose for you.

When we go home the sun has dropped behind
the trees. In the northern Pennsylvania dusk
a deer's eyes flash and I see
yours, glinting like hard coal in a pile
of ordinary rock. We sing silly songs
as if this were the trip from camp. I don't
ask any questions and no one gives me answers.

OVER THE RIVER AND THROUGH THE WOODS

Their house bloomed with Grandpa's stogies
and a drawerful of Old Spice jars.
Rhododendron blossomed in the yard.
Bean and barley soup steamed in the kitchen
in Blue Willow bowls. The wings of Pegasus
flew over the corner of Cedar Boulevard
and Cochran Road, gas was fourteen cents.
Along the Boulevard of the Allies
locust trees spread, promising Florida billboards,
blast furnaces below
along the river, every Sunday night,
Jack Benny on the radio, grandmother still blonde.

FIELD TRIP DAY

Fifth graders scrambled through maple leaves
red with the second frost of fall
and through oak leaves and over
an undergrowth of ferns and salal
to a cave in Frick Park.
I didn't understand
my grandparents' house was at the top
of the hill and I'd played on the swings
only a few hundred yards beyond the woods.
In Miss White's fifth grade class
I learned to be afraid of math
and to love the places I couldn't find
on my own. Another day
Mike and Susie ran ahead
through the room full of Greek statutes
as we looked for the dinosaurs
T Rex and some others whose names
have been changed by now.
I always got lost among the skeletons of prehistoric horses
sabre-tooth tigers and mammoths
and the green diorama with its giant ferns.
Back in class we had one hundred problems
to add, multiply, or divide.
Would Mike get his to Miss White's desk
before I did? Would my answers be right?
I was too nervous to think
of the spongy trail hugging the hillside
and the sack lunches we unpacked inside the cave
or the camels and pyramids in the dark boxes
at Syria Mosque where a hundred violins and trumpets
played triumphant Brahms and I studied Maria Revesz' old-
       country braids
circling her head in the seat in front of me.

Mike became an engineer
but overdosed on drugs.

Susie's a teacher somewhere in Ohio.
I still get lost looking for the dinosaurs at Carnegie Museum.
I still get nervous in a restaurant dividing the check.
My grandparents moved away, and now they're buried
in a cemetery I need more than a map to find.
I wonder what part of Miss White's job
she loved the best.

APRIL 18, 1955

I was not quite ten. My mother
took me to an allergy doctor
whose office was three rooms
behind glass and oak partitions
in the Jenkins Arcade. The doctor
scratched my skin with needles
and watched the lines redden
and swell. He told my mother
I should sleep with my bedroom
windows closed. After the appointment
we entered the elevator
with its brass scissors-grill gate
and rode down
past the mezzanine with its wrought-iron railing
to the long narrow lobby on the ground floor
and as we passed a newsstand
while I was still studying
the intricate black and white mosaics
under my feet
my mother said in a loud sad voice
"The smartest man in the world
just died." I glanced up
at the stack of *The Pittsburgh Press*
and my mother handed an old man a dime
even though we'd get the paper at home. We walked out
through revolving doors and across the street to Horne's.
We looked at the summer fashions in the windows
and waited for the bus. All the way home along
West Liberty Avenue I watched
people going in and out of shops
and stared at the wild-haired man
on the front page.
"He was Jewish," my mother said.

OVER THE HILL

Behind the taiga the tundra stretches
to an unknown ice.
I come over the hill
to a Siberian plain
where the smoke rises from chimneys
straight into the black Siberian sky.
I am coming home.
Coming home over the hill on a dark day
coming home in the cold over the hill
into a valley of light,
the light of ice and snow,
the light of white bean soup heating
on a Siberian stove.
I am coming over the hill
onto the plain of a Pennsylvania suburb
January or February
1958, 5:30 or 6 o'clock, the evening dark,
even Sputnik can't light up the dark,
the dark that comes before I'm home,
before dinner, before sleep,
before I can come over the hill,
so I belt the thick wool jacket tighter,
turn up the collar, wrap the hand-knit scarf
around my neck, wrap the Siberian memories
working my grandmother's fingers
one more time around my neck. I'm going home
over the hill to Siberia
following the icy asphalt
black as though sleds had smoothed it,
watching the shafts of smoke ascend
from the white icy valley, the Siberian suburb.

THE BUSINESSMEN'S LUNCH

In the Grill at the George Washington Hotel the murals in the
        popular-heroic style
of Thomas Hart Benton and the Federal Art Project were so large
that eating lunch at the Grill at the George Washington Hotel
was a visit to a tavern before the American Revolution,
and when I ate there every Saturday at noon with my father and
        his boss, Mr. Cowan,
I chewed my grilled cheese sandwich and stared at "The Old
        Oaken Bucket"
and thought that when Ben Cowan was a boy he lived like that boy
        in the murals,
bringing up water with that red pump handle, carrying the bucket
        back to his mother's hearty kitchen,
which smelled of brown ungarlicked beef, plain sugar-and-egg-rich
        loaf cakes.
The Grill at the George Washington Hotel smelled like black
wood and red tablecloths, smelled
like the low roar of men's conversations, but Ben Cowan
was the boy in colonial clothing, soft white shirt open at the neck,
blue knickers
buttoned below the knees, bare feet, a Dalmatian puppy
tagging along. What Ben Cowan knew about getting along in life
        without electricity
or indoor plumbing was what I really wanted to learn from the
        robust figures on the walls
and from Ben Cowan, too. He knew more than my city-bred
        father, so I sat still,
ate my sandwich and watched them swallow black bean soup and
        slabs of roast beef,
listened to them talk about the steel business and the business
of raising spotted dogs. With his round face and wide shoulders
Ben Cowan looked strong enough to carry buckets full of water to
        his mother's kitchen.
Even in his Saturday shirt and gabardine trousers he was strong
        enough
to teach my father to sell siding to the Army. This place proved

that everything they taught in school was true: George
            Washington,
Thomas Edison had really lived, had really changed our lives.
In the Grill at the George Washington Hotel I was certain
that these paintings were the only history I'd ever need,
and twisting the corners of the tablecloth, I listened
and finished my grilled cheese.

BEDFORD SPRINGS

Suddenly the spring sky has opened its jaws
to breathe pink wind across the tulips.
In the Blue Mountains strawberries start to grow
from the debris of crimson oak leaves. Snakes
slither out of holes
and yawn with the elegance
of crocuses. The blue warmth hugs the world
like a mother waking her child for school.
Suddenly the spring sky has opened its mouth
to taste the arbitrariness
of daffodils, the stickiness
of the red lake and its fresh skeletons,
their bones polished by the melting ice,
winter's roses crushed on the veranda
at Bedford Springs
where loudspeakers announce supper
with the Saber Dance
and the jaws of purple wind arrive
on the arms of the married lady, later,
when the lilacs have finished
and the lurid cosmologies of summer
appear at the red lake.
In the Blue Mountains
crayonned with corduroy,
a wistful blanket of summer
hisses at us from crevices. Eventually
the jaws that breathe pink wind
will hold the waking child
like a dying mother. Death
and gin weigh down our stickiness. At the red lake
the British play croquet. Young girls
with bittersweet nipples
study herpetology. The red lake
smells like chocolate. The candles
are blown out by the sun.

READING WILLIAM CARLOS WILLIAMS IN THE KITCHEN ON FOLKSTONE DRIVE

knotty
pine
cupboards
wrought
iron
handles

green
melamine
dishes
never
a carton
of milk
on the

yellow
formica
table
six
chairs

ice
skaters
at Cedar
Lake
a mural
we painted
every
night
for one
week

A CULTURAL HISTORY IN AMERICA

Brown yeast foams
in a cup of warm water,
a drop of honey
makes it explode.
Buttery onions,
parsley, rare tarragon:
all but their taste
disappears in brown dough.
Baking bread:
the ultimate activity
for women. The loaves
rise in clay pans
red from the iron-rich earth
my mother, a potter,
pointed out to me
in road cuts. My mother
never, to my knowledge,
made bread. She made
bread-plates.
And my grandmother
never made bread.
She bought hers
at the Waldorf,
where they specialized
in pumpernickel
and coconut whipped cream cake.
Am I a reversal
of all expectations
of cultural evolution?
Without a tradition
of bakers, no history
of women kneading and twisting
their souls into loaves
it's no wonder
I particularly love
to bake bread.

VAN GOGH AT THE CARNEGIE MUSEUM

for Audrey and Jane

Van Gogh had just arrived from Amsterdam.
Gaudy flowers, scenes
of sun-washed Provence

but all afternoon my friends and I
stared instead
at the dark peasants picking

at a plate of potatoes, studying
each others' faces the way
card players do. We lived

in kitchens with cardboard prints
of *Sunflowers* or *Boats on the Beach*
and now we glimpsed

the somehow secret possibilities
of a world our parents, fresh
from their own horrors, had tried

to spare us. But Van Gogh knew
the terror that lies
behind the choice of light.

L'ETRANGER

        Reading Albert Camus, 1962

Propped up on my pillow I'm reading
L'Etranger in French. By now
I understand well, there's no dictionary
beside the bed, I'm interested primarily
in the avant-garde philosophy,
existentialism, something
I only know is not what they teach us
in Mt. Lebanon. And just now
there has been something about Algeria
in the news: independence from France,
whether or not independence is a good idea,
whether or not non-European people can be
self-governing. I am vaguely interested
in that, and I do appreciate the opportunity
to read modern French, I have become
an avid follower of Jacques Prévert,
all of this is not anything like the way we live
in Mt. Lebanon. I turn on my side
and find a word I do not know, I hesitate
getting out of bed to find
the *Larousse*, but without it
I cannot read on, although I try, turning the pages
admitting nothing
makes sense.

THE BODY PUZZLE

Miss Parker moved stiffly with the skeleton she carried
in a box to our classroom.
She held the bones,
moved the arms and the hands
as if lifting a ruler
or blackboard eraser.
I was always uneasy,
knew that this object
had in fact been extracted
from the corpse of a person.
When she held the hook
screwed into its skull
I would watch her instead,
stiff and straight in the black dress
that concealed her body puzzle. Instead of the box

some days she would bring
a suitcase which opened to show us
a torso and head, made of plastic or rubber,
and each of the organs pulled out,
revealing beneath the position of others,
a body she could take apart and put back together
repack in the suitcase
and take to the next class.
And watching Miss Parker I questioned
her body, if it moved like the skeleton,
if it fit like the puzzle.

IN WESTERN PENNSYLVANIA

Her dreams were once rivers
gray rivers that curled through forests
like the early Monongahela
instead of factories she dreamed
a gray fortress in the forest
she dreamed stones grayer than stone
gray stones and gray trees
when there were enough stones
she built a fortress of her own
she curled through the forests
in silence like the river
she floated on bark stripped from gray tree trunks
floated on bark floated on stones dreamed
gray bark curled   rolling
like canoes from the last world

THE CASTLE AT CEDAR LAKE

The lake was a mine shaft. No one could say
how deep it was. We climbed the boulders knowing that,
to get a better view. The Castle stood beyond the trees,
turrets of gray stone above the pines. No one dared to go there.
We watched the wild ducks land on the lake
and ripple the black surface and our eyes shot

back and forth from the ripples to the flat gray
shale, the lakebed turned upright on the Castle,
and we yelled to the ducks to fly above the trees,
to report back on the safety of the Castle trail.
We did this until winter froze the surface of the lake
and the ducks waited in their liquid corners.

Some days we'd bring our little sisters with us
and when we'd get home they'd tell our mothers how
we'd taken them to Cedar Lake. We imagined it was Scotland,
there were raspberry leaves
curled and yellow, the only wild place we knew.

FAMILY

WHO I WANT FOR USHPIZIN IN MY SUKKAH, HOPING THEY CAN EXPLAIN IT ALL

Abraham and Sarah are where it starts for us.
Of course—don't we imagine ourselves
as a Biblical dynasty?
Abraham and Sarah. Abraham, the wise rabbi
from Veshey, a village
near Sereje, a village
near Vilna, in Lithuania.
A learned Litvak rabbi, all
intellect, like Abraham
who left Ur. And married Sarah.

Is that how the matchmaker fixed them up?
If there's a guy named Abraham, find him
a girl named Sarah?
Then, or course, this couple
have a son named Isaac.
(What do they think? That kids
are meant to be sacrificed?)
Isaac's a rabbi too, but he gets tired of the shtetl
and moves to Wales, where his sons

have gone into business. Then he leaves for America,
following other sons. After that
there are no more rabbis, but there are a few
in the family who learn a lot
and teach it to the rest of us.

Uncle Ellis gave me a miniature leather-bound *Macbeth*.
My dad taught Sunday school and studied Heschel.

Back to Isaac. Either he did it on his own
or the matchmaker couldn't find him
a suitable Rebecca. Anyway
he married Miriam
but we don't know much about her either.

(What do we know about
that other Miriam?
Not if she was even married
or had sons
or daughters, do we?)

Ushpizin: traditional Biblical or historical "guests" invited into a sukkah (booth) on the harvest holiday of Sukkot

1932

Harry Saul wraps the leather straps of *tefillin* boxes around his
    arm
Harry Saul recites his prayers next to his bedroom window
watches snow layering the branches of the sycamores outside his
    window
Harry Saul prays the way his father and his grandfather prayed
on winter mornings in Lithuania

although here Harry Saul is a merchant of Michelin tires
he lets his son wear the Michelin Man suit
lets his son parade around the streets of East Liberty advertising
    Michelin tires
like some fat rubber tire man I saw just last week
marching down Stone Avenue in Tucson Arizona

and he lets his daughter hitchhike with her girlfriend
hitchhike across the continent like any young man might
also he has taught his daughter Torah,
he has let her go to college

and here on a snowy January day Harry Saul is in his bedroom
    praying
and his wife has just walked downstairs to make the morning
    oatmeal and coffee
and there asleep in Harry Saul's favorite wing chair is a man
normally we might call him a burglar
he just came in off the streets for a warm place to sit
it's a January morning, there is snow on the sycamores
Harry Saul's wife is surprised, she's afraid, the man is large, and
    he happens to be black
he's asleep in his overcoat, his hands are nestled in its torn pockets

Harry's wife goes upstairs, she doesn't scream, she asks her
    husband what to do
Harry Saul tells his wife he is praying the way
his father and his grandfather prayed in Lithuania, he tells her
to leave him alone, so she walks downstairs

she walks past the man sleeping in her husband's wing chair

she thinks of her son, overheating in the tire suit
she thinks of her daughter, taking rides from strangers in Montana
she walks to the kitchen without waking the man
she makes the man oatmeal and coffee.

RETURN

San Xavier Del Bac

Under the porch light late brittlebush burned,
yellow on its gray wicks.
You'd finally come, that last spring,
to see the desert flower.

At the Mission flames sputter
on glass-coffined candles
below the statue of the dead priest.
The anniversary of the day you died,
and only here have I begun
to mourn you. Your voice

still stutters in the air.
You're the rabbi's grandson,
asking, *Who taught you to pray here?*
The flames are searching for the wrinkled recesses
where you might forgive me. But you're only saying
that I'd let this date
slip through my mind.
All I can hear

are the words you'd say each year,
Kaddish for your father, while I'd sit silent
on the hard pew, struggling
to learn the words I knew you wouldn't teach me,
as if to teach me meant you knew
someday I'd lose you.

At the Mission door
the brittlebush is burning,
yellow on its gray wicks.
Late spring, you've come
to see the desert flower.

BREAKFAST NOTES

     for Wendy

That day we climbed the power-line trail,
filling our baskets, staining hands and shirts,
dropping some when we wiped off sweat.
How you directed our children—
Hold your baskets level,
don't spill the berries, don't eat
too many—

how the briary hill
enclosed our labored breathing
how the soft rain came
to cool and clear the air

and you stirred juice on the wood stove
filling your house with purple steam.
The boiling
forced the sweet-sour smell
to enter our pores.

When you still lived here
you sent a card I framed
and hung above my breakfast table.
Fields of spring poppies, a stain of purple lupine
spread across the field—
like hot jam I spilled
across the yellow table. Again and again,
sister,
like sticky jam, sweet gold.

LOOKING FOR BARRACUDA

In sleep the water was Caribbean blue,
which I've actually seen, in which I actually swam
until I saw, through the goggles of my snorkel kit,
a barracuda. Despite the scare
that blue water recurs in dreams
surrounding me with a security the barracuda
took away.

                      When she was dying,
my grandmother heard my sister tell a story
about a shark bumping her leg as she swam
in the Atlantic. A few days later, the random
synapses confused in pain, my grandmother
cried out in her bed, a shark
is pushing on my leg. I was afraid,

wanted to push the shark out of the dying woman's dream.
In my own dream there are hidden caves
where the blue water comes up above sea level
and the air is more pure than above the open sea,
and black rock, wet with waves,
hides me from whatever fears I have.

When I am near the water I want a dramatic
and unforgettable experience to happen,
I want to suffer or enjoy a moment that may become
a poem, a myth, that will be like making love.
This has never happened. When I am near the sea
the moments, even the special ones, seem ordinary:

we buy shrimp and drink tequila, the gulls cluster
on the rocks where the fishermen have thrown the skin
and bones, the blue water is blue, and beautiful,
and we both say so.

                    Or there is a storm, but no one rushes

to save me, and I must take the intelligent actions
the situation requires, leaving, or fastening down the tent,
or moving higher on the beach, above the tides.

What I really want is to lead a precise life
        with room for emergencies. To look out onto the blue
        peaceful water
drinking tequila, looking for barracuda.

HUGGING YOU

for Ruth Saul

Hugging you
you seem so fragile
like a tiny porcelain
statue
that my arms are too strong for
as though I turned out male
by mistake
while you still think of me
as your little girl
we stand together
to you it must seem like forever
thinking
this is not my little girl
any more
and I
let the image of Mother drop
like a lover's shirt
to the ground.

MYTHOLOGY IN THREE PARTS

1. THE MUSIC BOX

It's broken and I want to fix it. I've had it since I was three and before that it was my mother's. Her favorite grandfather brought it to her from Europe, but it says "Made in Switzerland" in English on the inside of the lid.

This grandfather was always bringing my mother treasures from the nineteenth century: hand-made lace, a gold-and-silver tablecloth depicting an elaborate Eastern Orthodox wedding procession, a tiny sapphire-and-diamond ring, this music box. She keeps the lace put away in the back of some drawer, she uses the tablecloth for wedding and anniversary parties, but she gave me the ring and the music box.

When it worked the music box played *The Blue Danube Waltz* and *Lorelei*, played them on a brass cylinder dotted with tiny prick-points, which turned against fingers of steel that would lift and then fall with each note. Once there was a piece of glass fitted into the top of the box, but it's missing now, like one of the screws that held the works to the bottom of the box, and now the wood at the bottom of the box is broken too—I can't remember when that happened. Now it doesn't work at all, it must be overwound, the mainspring must be broken.

2. THE LORELEI

My mother was the one who first explained about
the *Lorelei*. I must have asked her, having heard the tune
only in the music box. The other melody, *Blue Danube Waltz*,

I'd heard in many other places. It didn't have
the mystery, the minor key.
                          This was before
I'd read the *Odyssey*, before I knew
anything about women

                              or men.

In the stories the Lorelei is a maiden
combing her wild golden hair
on a high cliff. Men on the Rhine below,
seeing her, seduced,
would wreck their boats and drown.

There are several stories. In each of them
the men are victims. In some
the Lorelei is too. The ghostly melody
is theirs, is hers.

3. THE BLUE DANUBE WALTZ

The Rhine is not a Jewish river. We
never understood virgins.

I do not try to understand the Rhine, only that once,
perhaps, William Friedman my great-grandfather

stopped to buy a music-box.
The Rhine is a river of dark spirits

he didn't need to understand.
William Friedman my great-grandfather

was a man of the Danube. The Danube
is a river of dancing. In white satin,

in velvet waistcoats, the men bowing,
the women circling beneath chandeliers

in a blazing ballroom, William Friedman,
in Budapest, in Vienna,

William Friedman waltzing.

LETTER TO MY GREAT-GRANDMOTHER IN KALUSZ

How old were you when Gedalia Ziegel—
his head full of dreams about America,
doing whatever he wanted—covered your mouth with kisses
and stroked your back with his soft hands
he didn't want to soak in the tanner's vats?
Three children he gave you on his return visits
before you left with him for Homestead.

How was Homestead different from Kalusz, Mudville?
Well, there were no pogroms.
(Only the Homestead Strike, before you came.)
But your daughter was raped
on the boat to America. (Oh,
she never told you.) Fannie was the proudest
woman I ever knew. I thought
she was a Queen, tall, dressed
in impeccable suits she made herself,
reigning over a kingdom
of toys. After that no man
could tell her what to do.

Who did you leave behind? Your mother,
who begged you not to go to America.
Four thousand miles west. You never saw her
again. Were you even twenty when you left?
Could you write to her after that? Who
would read your letters to her? Did you
write to her in Yiddish, or even Hebrew? Were you the one
who taught Fannie to read Hebrew? Were you the one
who sent Emalene to college?

In 1880 four thousand two hundred sixty six
Jews lived in Kalusz, including you. Sixty per cent
of the total town. The Carpathian mountains
rise to the west. In 1942 it was all over. Seventeen
somehow survived.

AUNT SARAH

Aunt Sarah set the table with her Wedgwood,
took inventory of the glassware,
shook the silver bell she used to ring the servants.
That is how the dinner would begin.
The silver bell was rung,
wine appeared in glasses.
It was always a holiday.
Aunt Sarah lit the candles,
passed her hands before the flames,
and bread would be blessed, and passed,
the silver bell would ring again,
and we would have beef sliced thin, asparagus,
potatoes covered with fresh parsley,
a still life on blue-and-white plates,
and then, after conversation, the bell would ring
and it would all be cleared away,
a cake would come in, covered with strawberries,
and coffee would be poured,
and Aunt Sarah would talk
about her night blooming cereus,
about the gardenias
she wanted to grow.

BIRTHDAY GIFT, MAY 22, 1977

    from my father: a portrait of his grandfather

Great-grandfather Isaac,
your half-closed eyes don't look at me
but make me feel you sat for the camera
daydreaming of its meaning,
preserving yourself
for your great-grandchildren.
Your eyelids are heavy like my father's
today in his hospital bed.
At fifty-eight his heart is weak.
You are the old man he will never be.

Today I am thirty-two.
Will I grow old?
Today I eat cake from my childhood memories
without regard to the cholesterol.
A week of sitting with anxious relatives
has made me fat. I know
I am my father's daughter.

My two children are at home.
By long distance telephone they tell me
they have wrapped the presents,
secrets they can scarcely hold inside.
Isaac from Lithuania, they are Kevin and Erica.
Will they know where they are from?

My father sits up in his hospital bed.
We toast life with his grape juice.
I eat the cold peas he has left on his tray.

We talk of real estate, the symphony,
politics. He is a man of the world
and expects me to be

and so I am.

THE WORDS OF THE PROPHET

> And they shall plant vineyards and drink the wine thereof;
> They shall also make gardens, and eat the fruit of them.
>
> And I will plant them upon their land,
> And they shall no more be plucked up
> Out of their land which I have given them...
>
> —Amos 9:14-15

In our suburban yard my mother grew
strawberries and green beans,
enough to freeze

There was a sour cherry tree for pies
and a sweet cherry that, planted alone,
could not bear fruit.

When he came home from work, my father
would take my mother by the arm,
"check out the back forty,"

strolling the twenty steps
to the arbor of Concord grapes
at the property line

overlooking the hollow of Cedar Creek
where I could pick wild raspberries
and swing on monkey vines

and in his volume of the prophet Amos
my father would only scribble

"We're all dreamers"

LETTER TO MY GRANDMOTHER WHO HAS BECOME BLIND

    for Emalene and Erica

Grandma, here's a photograph I took of you and Erica
When we came to see you. Even if
You can't see it very well, I know you'll like it.
Erica just played a Bach concerto for you—

She holds her violin under her right arm,
And with her left hand holds your hand,
You and Erica are looking at each other
With beautiful smiles, Grandma,

Make them tape this picture to your wall.
Don't believe them when they say you can't see it.
Put this picture on the wall—
You'll know it's there.

INTERSTICES

Between white birch trunks
in some Galizianer forest
I see in the lines of my genealogy:

A young man in officer's uniform
Honor Guard to Franz Josef,
conscripted against his will.
His uniform made his family proud,
offered them protection. His wife
divorced him, he was gone for so long
and she at twenty
needing only his warm body beside her
knowing she could not have it
supported her children
as a kosher caterer
to the Jewish Baron.

Coal fields and black stone walls
in Lithuania
in Wales
in Dunlo, Pennsylvania.
A man named Isaac
I know from a photograph.
I know his wife's name: Miriam.
I imagine them in the Baltic capital
stretched out on a large white bed
on a warm day, making love
and talking about England.

A man at the next table
moves his hand softly
up and down a woman's back.
I can see by their faces
their histories are different.
All our histories are different.
We'll never know the names

the stories
or the touch of love
the soldier once brought his bride
or her loneliness
late at night.

FOR KEVIN'S TENTH BIRTHDAY

This year we can't hike in the Canyon
and I'll miss seeing the red rocks with you,
our dropping steadily down
to the midway oasis of lush grapevines
where we picked tangy fruit
and washed our tired feet
in a blue stream.

It's easy for a mother
to feel sentimental when her son is ten.
I want to resist that, to feel as hard as the rock
we climbed together
but like the redwall limestone
shaped by centuries of wind and water
and tinted by iron from the rock above,
you and I have worn into each other
and taken on colors
we didn't have before.

I choose objects and places
to teach you about our world.
I want you to love its vastness
and its detail.
I point out fossils I can barely see,
ancient snails lying open to the desert sky.
We spot hawks and eagles as they soar
from rim to rim.
You marvel, shout, gasp—
learning. But for every thing
that I show you
you focus my eyes
on two.

WHAT I'M HOPING TO FIND

Why are you going to Hungary? he asks me.
What do you hope to find? Tell me,
What would it take to make you happy?
For your ancestors to sit up in their graves
and tell you how it really was? I guess,
I stammer, that's what I want
but since they won't, I want
the next best thing: finding
their stories on carved stone
and archived in small print.
Name of midwife: Friedman Re'zi
Name of circumciser: Bermann Lipot
Name of godfather: Reichard David, wine trader.
Was the midwife an aunt? Was she trained
or merely the sister-in-law
trying to help—
or to control?
Was the godfather, the wine merchant,
a friend of the gambling father
who came to America to avoid his debts?
What did the house at Kazinczy Utca 515
look like? What sort of people would
have lived there? I'm looking for the rest
of the stories I know:
the exposition, the prequel. Yes, I tell him,
I want them to sit up in their graves
and tell me
my truth.

DAYENU

       Hungary, 1997, for my mother

If we had eaten dobos torte and strudel by the Danube
       Dayenu
If we had danced to tunes of gypsy violinists
       Dayenu
If we had stood to pray in the synagogue on Dohány Utca
       Dayenu
If we had stood at the gate of Annie's house in Cégled
       Dayenu
If we had seen the gardens in her courtyard
       Dayenu
If we had stood in the painted synagogue in Nyiregyhaza
And listened to a survivor of Auschwitz
Teach us our history
       Dayenu
If we had drunk the wine of Tokaj grown on grapestakes cut by
    Friedmans
       Dayenu
If we had chanted psalms below the blue ark in the Tokaj ruin
       Dayenu
If we had followed the lumber wagon drawn by horses on the road
    in Porosko
       Dayenu
If we had photographed the blessing hands on graves of Friedman
    Cohanim
       Dayenu
If we had found the grave of Basha bas Shmuel, who must be your
    grandfather's sister
       Dayenu
If we had said Kaddish at the cemetery in the cornfield
       Dayenu
If we had found your father's birth record in the archive in Ujhely
       Dayenu
But we read the record of his baby brother, nameless, dead at 10
    days

And "the father has emigrated to America,"
                Dayenu
And we found, completely by chance
The cemetery funded by the mysterious wine-merchant
Who was your grandmother's stepfather
The cemetery, perhaps,
Where your grandmother is buried
The inscription above the white portal
"Go in peace."
                Dayenu. It would have been enough.

Blessed are You, Who gives life to the dead.

Notes:

"Dayenu," which means "it would have been enough" in Hebrew, is a repetitive song sung with great energy and enthusiasm at the Passover Seder.

"Blessing hands...Cohanim" refers to the image of the hands lifted in the priestly blessing inscribed on the gravestones of Jewish men with the family status of "Cohen" (priest)

I AM TRYING TO UNDERSTAND

      Cegléd, Hungary, July 1997

I am trying to understand a woman
who chose handmade lingerie
over America
who returned to her husband
five years before their son
would be shot

Whose hand sewed the yellow star
onto her coat?

I am trying to understand how, four years after
they returned from the camp
a man and a woman are smiling at the lake.
They are there with her cousin and their friends
Six people enjoying their vacation

What have the healing waters at Heviz
been able to wash away?

I am trying to understand
what a woman who has lost her son can think
when she plants four-o-clocks and daisies
in her garden
where they once sat, reading

I am trying to understand how a woman like that
can plant any garden at all
how she could tend her grapevines

The Communists allowed them one room in their house
that had been a wedding present from her father
the house confiscated in 1944
"Jewish owner: title cleared"
Which room did they receive?
Had anyone kept

the lace cloths, the crocheted bedspread?
I am trying to understand—
Did she want them back?

I am trying to understand
how they told her that her son was dead.
Did it happen at his school?
Were they taken to the camps the same day,
or the next?

I am trying to understand
why I am standing in Annie's courtyard
Why I bend down to smell the tarragon
and chervil growing among rocks
Why I photograph bunches of fat grapes
Why I think it could be mine

HARMADIK GENÉRACIÓ MAGYAR

Balatonfüred július 2004

*"Az itthonról elszármazott vagy második -harmadik
generációs külföldön élo magyar..."*
*"The artists from home or second and third generation
from abroad-living Hungarian..."*

from *Müertö* (Budapest July 2004 *Art
Conoisseur* magazine)

Here I am, having grown up
third-generation American. Two grandparents
Litvak, one Galizianer,
one Magyar. My grandfather, born Friedman Miksa
in Sátoraljaújhely (where Kazinczy wrote
and Kossuth rallied for independence),
left me stories, and my mother
has given me the lace
her Hungarian grandfather had given her,
hoping to make her a suitable Hungarian matron.
And here am I, following the stories
and the lace, eating *halasylé* and *gyulas*,
everything with *paprika,*
drinking *a finom bor* and *palinka.*

Here am I, *harmadik genéració magyar,*
not a stranger to this country
of nineteenth-century buildings, domed and yellow-stuccoed,
lace-curtained windows opening
to the sun. Not a stranger
to the vineyards, grapes ripening for wine,
or to the gardens full of apricot and pear trees,
the fields of sunflowers,
forests of chestnut and oak.

Harmadik genéració magyar,
in the market I ask for and receive

harom gombas, three white mushrooms
to cook with gold-and-red paprika,
squash, and shiny purple onion.
At the *posta* I ask for *harom harminc-forint* stamps,
to complete the postage I need
to send three postcards
airmail to America.

My grandfather called his Grandmother Friedman
"a big strapping Hungarian woman."
Accent on Hungarian.
Fani Schonberger Friedman Schlanger
of Porosko. We called the woman in the photograph,
made at a studio in Varanno,
"the iron lady," frightened by her severe hat
and what appeared to be a scepter.
An Orthodox Jew, covering her hair in modesty,
100% Hungarian. The scepter
is actually a parasol, perhaps
the photographer's prop.

On the bus in Budapest
I look at faces, ask myself
who would have turned me in
in 1944. I walk down narrow ghetto streets,
harmadik genéració magyar,
knowing that Enny's husband Pal, whose name
can be found in the *Aranyalbuma*
published to celebrate the service of Jewish officers
in the First World War, was conscripted
into a Labor Battalion, Enny deported
to Auschwitz, then Buchenwald, their son
shot into the Danube. On the lawn next to our villa
stands a monument
to the Hungarian heroes, a soldier
of the Second World War, exhausted

from what duty? My grandfather
made the right choice,

left behind the formal kissing of hands,
and his sister Enny, perhaps, chose wrong.
But still I am here,
third-generation Hungarian,
according to the art review.

UNCLE IZ

Watermelons were the special treat he brought
for the Fourth of July, when the family crowd could eat it up
so it wouldn't be squeezed into our old refrigerator. Once a year
we'd drive through a maze of streets
through tree-lined neighborhoods of mansions
to visit his grocery, and bring home
a bag of fresh peas I'd sit on the porch
and shell, all the while my mother
telling me what a treat they were,
and how Uncle Iz got up at three in the morning
to go to the Farmers' Market where special people like him
could buy these things. The peas
plinked into the shiny colander, bright green
filling the dull aluminum, covering the small holes,
I liked to pick them up a little and let them rain down
over my fingers, and toss the opened pods into a pile
on the Sunday comics at my feet. The Select Food Market
put a mink stole on my aunt's shoulders, but for me
it yielded treasures more valuable than pearls:
fresh peas, strawberries, watermelons, a taste
that meant *I've got an uncle who knows the secret.*

GRANDMA EM'S PRAYERBOOK

Grandma Em didn't pray much, as far as I knew.
When I'd see her at Beth Shalom on Rosh Hashanah
her sister Fannie would be praying
but Grandma would be talking to her friends.
She worked every Saturday in her store,
she'd stopped lighting Shabbos candles.
Imagine my surprise when, after she died,
we found a new gray *Mahzor* next to her chair, open to a prayer she'd chosen
to read, a year before she died
on the last day of the Jewish year.
She'd sent her aide to Pinsker's
to buy that book.
And then, a few years later, my mother
found this ivory and leather-bound book,
a prayerbook, in Hebrew and English,
published in Frankfurt in 1895—the year Em had been born—
the Ten Commandments on the cover
held as Moses might have held the tablets,
at the bottom, with the tops spreading apart.
Leaves cut out of ivory surround the tablets.
When did Em get this prayerbook? A wedding gift?
Nothing is written
on the inside cover.
When did she use it?
What were her prayers?

THE CERAMIST

> (Judy Chicago wrote of visiting the
> kitchen/bedroom/basement studios of women artists)

"I'm going down the cellar to eat worms"
Mama's frequent threat to her brood
husband four children constantly
needing
her escape meant to cut into our
skin
and in the cellar
in a windowless corner
never more than three
inches
from the washing machine
the white kiln-glow peeked out
searing into my skin "my mother is an artist"
old rolling pins in an old
kitchen cabinet
dusty and gray with the
clay pies
"I'm going down the cellar to eat worms"
bitter joys
the sculpture and the painting given over to
a few bad cups
strange awkward unstackable relish bowls
always talk of building a large lamp
modern
(ah but I too
was bitten
made small statues and boxes
studied art in junior high school
worked in a studio with windows on a second floor
gave it all up for a
male profession)
Mama still works in a windowless
cellar three inches from the

washing machine
hangs up her oilcloth to dry
above old kitchen cabinets painted with unfired glazes
and the white hot peek-hole still registers
that affirmation
My mother is an artist.
Now she begins to
feel
lines textures
colorations
Now she begins to
share
the worms must be gone down the drain with the
slip
I wish for her a studio sharing the
sky
without a
washing machine.

TANTE

She stood tall, regal
silver hair piled into a bun,
wearing an elegant suit of red
or bright yellow. Queen
of the Toy Store. Each of us
could choose one gift, making
the morning's entertainment.
In her hall, the wallpaper showed
a lion spitting a fountain from its mouth.
In the kitchen the floor was
a giant checkerboard, polished
black and white, and on the counter
warm strudel from her Hungarian cook.
Her chairs had tight round cushions
we kept sliding off. She kept photos
on a corner desk: a sporting man, reeling in
a large fish on the deck of a yacht,
photos I'd later associate with Hemingway,
but he was her husband. Later,
when you pressed her, she would talk:
the Jewish man she watched as he was
eaten by a pig, the soldiers cheering.
The ship to America, being raped.
At ninety, she still keeps books by hand,
checking tiny numbers in black ink.

THE CHALLAH COVER

    for Erica

No one will give me household presents
since I'll never marry, you said
so to prove that isn't true
I've given you the challah cover
a wedding present to your father and me
from the German woman I hated as babysitter
but loved when I learned
she was the grandmother of a friend

Margaret Frankel embroidered it
in cross-stitches, a loaf, the word "Shabbat"
I haven't used it as often as I'd hoped
You're the one who bakes fresh challah every Friday
You're the one who sings the blessings
with the other women in your group

We braid the strands of soft dough according
to the intricate diagrams in our new book
five strands to twist together
a pattern new to each of us

Here, this strand crosses two to its left
Then, lift this one over the two on its right

Our lives braid together
in this dough.

TRANSYLVANIA

My ancestors in Transylvania
must have shivered during thunderstorms
when the lightning lit the towers of the Count's castle
and seemed to float above the treetops

and when they moved from their forest hamlets
first to the yellow-stuccoed town of Ujhely
and then to the big city, Kolosvar
they might have thought that they'd escaped
from the terror of forest darkness

but the roofs of Kolosvar
echoed, in their rows and rows of slate-gray peaks,
the shapes of nature, granite crags and pine trees,
and here it was not the Count
but the Prince himself
who could control a doctor's life
threaten him

so he would change his religion
change his name
and flee to Mexico,
taking his fine cigars.

GRANDPA'S COUSIN

Pal Czinner 1890-1972

From fin-de-siècle Budapest you went to Vienna,
studied philosophy and literature,
then Shakespeare in Berlin.
You married a girl from near my grandma's hometown,
a Galizianer to your proud Hungarian family,
an actress you would direct again and again,
in German, then in English.
You and Bergner escaped to London in 1933
beating Hitler's deadlines.
She played the gamine Rosalind when you cut *As You Like It*
to ninety minutes. Later
touring in America
you stepped out on hotel room bills
and your cousin, my grandfather,
for some reason didn't take my mother to see you.
During the War, afraid of being sunk,
Bergner wouldn't take a ship
across the Atlantic
so you stayed with her
in Canada and Hollywood.
You were friends with Remarque,
and in his will, James Barrie
left your wife 10,000 pounds.
You've been outed on the Net
and the Mormons claim to have baptized you.
You look just like my grandfather did
when he was thin,
but with a telling scar.

TRANSCRIBING THE NYIREGHAZA HUNGARY HOLOCAUST MEMORIAL

These are the names...
Married couples
.....Lajos
.....Lajosne
.....Samu
.....Samune
whole families
Es Csaladja
Muller L. Es Csaladja
Dr.
Ozv. (the widow of...)
These are the names.
None of them belong to me.
Inscribed on pink stucco
all of them belong
to all of us.

IN MY STUDY

This room could be
a primitive epitaph for my life
Anyone could find here
the blessings of memory,
collections from the downslope
of jilted dreams:

shelves of poetry, fiction,
handwritten journals, and magazines
hiding fragments of my work.

The walls will bombard the visitor
with more remote blessings of memory:
the "ancestor worship" photographs
and the one of my offspring, hanging with ropes
from a Yosemite cliff face.

African artifacts will deceive,
given to me by my brother
but I admit an affinity
to the green, red and black cloth
bearing the proud figure of a woman
and the words I thought meant "To our health!"
inscribed in a hybrid language.

MAY THIS CHILD

    a blessing for my soon-to-be-born grandchild who turned
    out to be Emerson

May this child
love to smile,
love to pick up rocks
on walks in the desert
and make Papa carry them home
in his backpack.
May this child grin
at the mother quail
leading her young
from underneath the palo verde trees,
laugh at long-eared jackrabbits
that run when they hear his footsteps,
recognize the saguaros for playmates and elders
hold out his hands to catch the raindrops,
catch snowflakes on his tongue.
May this child read Sendak and Seuss,
read Neruda,
may Aiyana read
every Harry Potter book
out loud to this child.
May this child dangle his toes
in the water of desert creeks,
mountain waterfalls,
the ocean that will connect him
to the entire world,
cuddle cats and play with Popo,
dance on his Mama's toes,
dance to the music in his own head,
whistle Mozart,
sing in a minor key.
May this child play with clay
and paint and learn to weave.
May this child learn to be patient.

May this child learn to love the world and all that is in it.
May this child live in a world at peace.

THE VISIT

      August 2007, visiting my mother

All week long we watch the news unfold
The miners lost beneath the surface
The rescuers themselves die
This morning's headline
"Utah mine rescuers admit defeat"
You can't remember
Your memories no more retrievable
than those men trapped in the rock
A TV show about cats and dogs reminds you of someone...
Slowly you speak the words...
"Minneapolis—is it a granddaughter—a great-granddaughter
—something to do with animals"
My daughter, a vet, who lived with you each summer.
The transparent hoya flowers, clustered
In the Fibonacci sequence you never knew about
so hadn't used as you pressed their petals into
the clay bowl you're making
Nitroglycerine
In a pocket of the earth
In a velvet bag in your pocket

THE OIL PAINTING

Through the crack, rip in the old canvas
The old Europe leaks
The intense mystery of a childhood
In the shadows
The scene a bridge over a canal
And the narrow joined canal houses of Holland
And the odd figure walking toward the bridge, away from me.
Holland, not my grandmother's unremembered Kalusz with her
        grandmother's cow and peach trees,
Not my grandfather's remembered Hungary of bandit uncles and
        wealthy doctor uncles with stashes of cigars he stole,
A mystery that was just a painting my grandmother must have
        liked, so she picked it to hang in her living room
where I could study it as though it had something to tell me
And now it has cracked and torn
But I need it more than ever
Need to discover what is under the cracks
What can emerge, born from bridges over canals.

THE GARDENS

In Porosko my ancestors were tenant farmers
hired other laborers to work the fields
which Jews were not allowed to own

Wheat, cabbages, corn perhaps
They had orchards of plums
peaches, apples

Always the flowers
four-o-clocks
daisies
clematis
wild blooms

in well-kept rows
the green effusion
of grape leaves

Along the river and in every yard
grew willows
Even on the gravestones
graceful willows
watered like the Tree of Life
promised a rooted soul

PAPRIKA

My grandfather longed for Hungarian goulash—
a soup he could barely remember,
the taste of paprika unlike anything
in America. His Galizianer wife
wasn't about to even try
to make it for him. They fought about it—
she'd sneer, recalling something greasy
he'd once gotten her to taste
in the Hungarian restaurant on Second Avenue.

The spice he searched for in his life
hangs in strings across the grocer's window
on Castle Hill in Budapest, looking
like chile ristras here at home.
I can't wait to taste the real thing
and I do—goulash soup, paprika fish
with and without sour cream.
My mother sneers—the fish is full of bones
but I'm warmed by the rich red sauce
as hot as chile, and sometimes
by slices of crisp green pepper
with a bite and a lingering fire
stronger than any jalapeno.

Oh, my heritage is in these plants
that traveled from Mexico to Spain
and then to Hungary,
that travel back to Arizona now,
seeds tucked into an empty film can.

I'll cook the soup that Grandpa dreamed of,
grow this spice in Grandpa's memory.

THE SILENCE AT NIGHT

You won't talk about it. You go every day
to visit your father, you say that much,
and that you'll bring him home tomorrow,
or that he's worse, tomorrow you'll take
your aunt to see him. You won't say
what's wrong, or how his eyes look
gazing out from hospital sheets, or what,
if anything, the old man eats
from the speckled plastic tray.
So there's nothing I can tell you
about those days when I visited my father
and tried to talk to him
about the ordinary affairs of the world,
listened to the slowness in his voice.
I can't tell you about the nights
when it was so hot in my room,
how at 3 a.m. I had to go and sit
on the green carpet in the living room
because it was as lush as early spring
because it was the color of the cold peas
I'd picked off his tray after dinner
because my mother and I couldn't talk about it
even when she came to ask me why I couldn't sleep.
I wanted to shake the words out of life
without speaking to another human being
because the sight of my father dying
meant nothing to anyone but me.

NASHIM B'MIDBAR / WOMEN IN THE DESERT

THE WAY TO GO

      for Hu:si

In your language and mine
the translation is the same:
the way to go.
In English, from your word
they say *custom,*
from mine, *the law.*
The root of each word
to walk
words of two peoples who walk
in two deserts, naming
sky, stone,
water,
the trees.
To some interpreters
your word means
quaint, picturesque people
who can't continue
to live that way
and my word means
quaint, hated people
who follow rigid rules and refuse
salvation.

Himdag, halacha.
Neither of us walks
directly on the trail

but we are trying
to walk together.
The way to go.

We are trying
to walk together.

IN OUR LANGUAGE

Four birds with wide black wings extended
in our language we call them buzzards
to the west, four more,
wings folded, all eight
facing something in the mountains to the south
the head and empty skin of a butchered cow
and all its bones above it
laid out in the form they had in life
in our language we call it skeleton
in our language we call it mystery
beyond the mountains there are more mountains
beyond the mountains there are cows
coyotes javelina
lions
in our language these things are ordinary
the brown and white hide of the dead cow
the white bones of the dead cow
in our language these things are unspeakable.

FROM THE DESERT

All afternoon the rain moirés the glass,
turns the violent grass outside
into a desert of footprints.
I've been thinking of you, Wendy, of how

slowly you might be lifting the silkscreen
from your newest prints,
the way Pablo Casals is lifting his arm
across the Bach that cools this August afternoon.

Tomorrow fresh frogs will leap out of the new ponds,
this neighborhood suddenly a landscape of lakes.
The hills behind my house are green, like your West
        Virginia hollows.
Wendy, do you remember this place,

the prickly pears red in the rain,
tawny mesquite beans hanging on the trees?
I dream you've left your footprints in the Comobabis,
that the frogs bellowing are the cattle on your farm,

that my life is as clear as Bach, yours
as true as the calendars you're printing.
You lift the screen above July: a woman stands
by a hedge of hollyhocks. Rain leaves its film

across the window. The mountains
have washed away. And our dreams,
Wendy, will you print them
on the next page?

WHITE HORSES WEST OF ANEGAM

Keeping an even speed,
I sing to myself
and think about stopping,
perhaps by a stock pond,
hoping to photograph cattle,
or the wind on the pond,
or nothing.

The white horses appear so suddenly I forget
I've seen them on this road before. Once,
driving at night, I would have hit one
but as I turned a shallow curve
my headlights lit its neck
and it glowed
translucent as a *Shabbas* candle in a darkened room.

Today, there are three of them.
Standing like three ghosts next to the trees,
they swing their tails while they watch me drive by,

and I take a breath and know
that if I'd only stopped
and held out my camera,
I would have stayed
in unconditional surrender.

FOUR POEMS FOR GEORGIA O'KEEFFE

I

BLACK IRIS, 1926

When you tried to find
the black iris bulb
but could not
you gave us instead
black velvet breath
a tongue of silk
in the palette of dried blood
white satin folds
a tunnel
to that unknown place
that holds, in your garden,
every moment we might have tried
not to find.

II

COW'S SKULL, 1931

The bleached skull of a desert cow.
Split, the skull is two hands.
Long fingers of its jaw
invoke
the depths of your country you wanted
the men to notice.
You, the woman
who knew cows.

III

PELVIS III, 1944

Like raw porcelain
pulled by the hands
of a distracted potter
what you have chosen remains
sky from the bottom
of the world's
last well.

IV

BLACK BIRD SERIES, IN THE PATIO IX, 1950

It rises
even within the peace
of your own stuccoed walls
a precise black wedge
covers the clouds
until you see
how it will always move
out of your dreamed
horizon.

ARIZONA ANGEL

Could the Aztecs have known angels
living, as they did, in a place of heat,
the sun breathing fire with horned flowers
the rain feeding the jungle
the press of fleshy leaves on everyone's shoulders?
No wonder the pyramids, the hearts torn
from breathing bodies narcotized by chocolate.
No angels could diminish the heat, would have survived.

But some mother, her son
chosen as the next offering, exchanged
a quick kiss for a long walk north,
toward a land of tiny leaves, little rain,
a land where the angel sun would whisper
the names of springs to keep her world alive.

Notes:

This poem is based on ideas contained in the works of some anthropologists and historians, in Leslie Silko's *Almanac of the Dead*, and among some O'Odham people, that the O'Odham and some other inhabitants of Southern Arizona/northern Mexico were refugees from the violence of Aztec society.

Specific images also come from the O'Odham etymology of key place names in the Tucson area:

ali shon: Tohono O'Odham "little spring," origin of name Arizona
shon: a base or foundation; the trunk or stump (or a plant); the source or beginning; an ancestor; a spring (Saxton dictionary)—root of *Ali Shon*, "Arizona" and *Chuk Shon*, "Tucson"

DESERT CHARCO

      for Kevin and Erica

most of her water
has evaporated
into the sky
where it turned blue
and followed the wind

      into the mountains
      and out to the ocean

the rest of it
drained into the earth

only a few feet down
the moist earth
feeds the roots

      of mesquite
      and palo verde
      and saguaro

not much water in her now
just enough

      the highest peak reflects
      on her brackish surface

      an acknowledgment
      of the full moon

she tries to hold on
to memories of summer
thunderstorms

when her children stood

next to her
and looked past the surface

      but the reflection
      wasn't strong enough
      to interest them

she guards the small pool that's left
in case they come back

CORNCOBS

    visiting Tonto National Monument

In the ruin I held a corncob
stripped of its kernels
eight hundred years ago, the cob
small as my little finger. I felt

invited there. I touched
the handprints women left
on a kitchen wall,
pressed my fingers

into curves
varnished by smoke.
Kneeling beside
a broken metate

I rocked,
listening for songs
in the corn. They left
without teaching anyone

those songs. They left
only these grinders of stone,
and corncobs,
corncobs.

PICKING PEAS

    (every fall I plant *Tohono O'Odham* peas, an heirloom
    seed marketed by Native Seeds/Search, Tucson)

On this first hot day of spring I am picking the rest of the peas
so I can turn over the ground for potatoes.
Endless pairs of plump pods go into a plastic bag, always
more hiding behind thin flat leaves. Another bag
holds the dry brown seeds from the bottom of the vines,
next year's crop. These peas
are descendents of seeds the priests
and the secret leftovers of my own people
brought to the O'Odham 450 years ago
from their mothers' gardens in Toledo. These peas
hold into the warm desert spring, grow thick
and tall and bear thousands of mealy seeds
that taste like history.

Slowly I step along the row, pulling off ripe swollen pods,
leaving the thin ones never to grow to harvest.
There are still a few white flowers, too, along the top
but I will pull them all out, later. These decisions
must be made. When I think I have harvested
everything ready in this section, I yank the vines
from their roots, as the Conversos were yanked
from theirs, and find
more full pods dangling, ones I would have missed

and think about all the other things I miss
because I need to replace everything
before its time. Fearing
that the last plump pod I miss will be the one
that by genetic miracle is the sweet one, cross-bred,
I could love the most.

THE MAN WHO DIDN'T LIKE TO TALK

It doesn't seem as far as my father came,
and his brothers, one or two at a time,
steerage from Danzig. Some with their wives,
the others still boys, just as glad
to leave the old rabbis behind.
To take a train across America,
that's not as far as a ship
in cold Atlantic winds.
But the stars they saw must have been as bright
as the stars above the desert.

I'm glad, too, to leave them all behind
in Pittsburgh: the women who talk while they cook,
won't stop, who's gotten married,
whose baby's sick. And the men,
even the ones who don't argue about God
are arguing business, who sells
pots and pans for less, who got hired
by that new guy, Kaufmann, at his fancy store. Sure,

I'm in business, too, pots and pans
even, but there's no one here
I have to talk it to. The Indian men
buy for their wives in San Miguel
and up in Santa Rosa, and they
don't say much, just the few words
they know in English
or think I know in Papago. Just enough

to choose a pot, figure the price of some cloth,
add a can of coffee and maybe a new ax handle,
something for himself. Sometimes one brings his wife,
they'll talk a little in their own language,
but soft, sometimes breathing up the words
so I don't have to listen. Back home

they thought I was strange not talking much.
Here no one cares. Maybe even like me better
than that other trader who asks too many questions.
I sell my pots and pans
and drive the wagon back to Tucson. Takes two days
but when I stop at night I watch the stars
like my father did on that ship.
I lie so the mountain covers the moon
and cuts a slice into the sky so I know I'm still on land.
I lie on my back till I'm part of that slice.
Then I talk to the black sky.

PERSEID LOVE POEM

I can't remember what you said
my ears heard nothing that you said
the night the Perseid meteor showers
would come, if the clouds would clear away
so I looked up into the sky
hoping to see some shooting stars
some kind of omen or at least good luck
but my eyes were too full of clouds to see any stars
and you were holding me against you and I just said
can't talk about it now, and turned around

And the shooting stars were visible that night
when I got home
in the back yard
on a chair on the deck
looking northeast
just like it said in the *Field Guide to the Night Sky*
suddenly there were two, three, and then streaks of meteors
with tails like jet planes
and my eyes traced the points of Casseiopeia
and Pegasus and Ursa Minor
and my lips repeated: Andromeda, Andromeda
like it could bring you back
like it could send you away.

BURNING STORIES

At seven, before sunset,
alone in a yellow lawn chair,
I am burning the dream

of the man I love.
I have just finished reading
an amusing story, written,

it would appear,
by a Russian dissident,
who has come to this country

although he is neither Jewish
nor an outspoken scientist,
something about an ordinary man

and his peculiar wife.
Although the air
has stopped being warm

the squirrel-cage cooler fan
still taps and wheezes
and the light

has just decided
to change, the sky
has taken on the yellow glare

of the atomic explosion
of palo verde blossoms
with mesquite pollen.

He warned me
not to write about him,
and I promised.

When he started

telling me his dreams
it was only a way

into morning conversations
but his dreams became
an extension

of my own stories,
found their way
into journal pages

and scribblings
on yellow pads.
In the dream I've just tossed

into the fire,
he is always naked,
walking around town

the way he always does
until he finds
a conversation. To start

the conversation, I had to write it down.
In the story the man
and his strange wife,

who like us have forgotten to marry,
never talk, slip into routines
of coffee, breakfast,

choose each other
they way people choose
a comfortable cafe.

Today I searched without success
for a children's book
where a drunken Irish poet

once drafted a few lines
after we'd made love
for twenty-four hours,

before I'd sent him out
into the passionate sunset.
Ordinary people make these sacrifices.

So I crumple the sheets
of yellow dreams, burn your nakedness
in a real fire, go back to being alone.

THE DARK AGES RETURN TO THE TUCSON WRITERS' CONFERENCE

December 1988

Dark medieval castles, Europe. Death. No point to it. Even the bird is dead. Dead horns of a deer, dead faces, dead cloth. The glittering red cloth of a cardinal, dead as the mask. Red of blood, flowing down stone steps, flooding whatever is left below. Night is falling but isn't it always night, even when the sun is out? Wasn't it always dark in the Dark Ages?

TO LILITH: CONSIDERATIONS ON WOMEN, MEN, CHILDREN, AND THINKING FOR YOURSELF

> "Oppressed Hair Puts a Ceiling on the Brain"
> —Alice Walker

It's the wild hair that draws me to you.
Snakes, they say, as they said later of Medusa.
My mother lifts her hand to my forehead, brushes away
the gray waves falling over my eye. Last year, she says,
when your hair was short, it was
so cute. I am forty-five years old but she's hurt
when I tell her I didn't like my hair last year.
I like it now. I like the strength of hair,

power that comes from hair
not being oppressed. Comes from
not having to bother. Comes from saying,
This is who I am. Take it or leave it.

They say you ate your children.
Well, some say I gave mine away.
Of course I never thought their father'd tell them
not to see me. But now they see me, now we talk,
and my daughter, who's shaved off all her hair,
is even more like you than I am.

Well, what it really was
had nothing to do with hair. It's just
that you left Adam, and that worried him
and a lot of other men. My problem, though,
is how hard it is to leave. But I find
that a man who likes my wild hair
I have no need to leave.

Aviva says your opposite is Esther. That's the part of me
I never owned. Oh, I once imagined
I could seduce Khrushchev, who looked like my grandfather,
to end the cold war. But my beautiful sister,

who had straight hair in those days,
was the one dressed as the Queen each Purim.
I was wild-haired Ahasueras, with a beard.
I didn't know you, Lilith, then. If I had,
you're who I would have been,
if my mother'd let me.

Of course, in the end the point was
you said God's name aloud.
You felt equal not only to Adam,
but to God. On a first-name basis!

Aviva says your revolt is "intrinsically Jewish."
Medusa, Lamashtu, Labartu, archetypal sisters,
did not revolt. Although my mother never thought so

what I wanted my children to learn
was just that: *Revolt* is the heritage we give you.
Lilith, I always hoped my daughter
would be like you!

Sources:

Alice Walker, *Living by the Word*, New York, Harcourt Brace Jovanovich, 1988.

Aviva Cantor, "The Lilith Question," in Susannah Heschel, *On Being a Jewish Feminist*, New York, Schocken, 1983.

SONG FOR MIRIAM

> "Then Miriam the prophetess, Aaron's sister, took a
> timbrel in her hand,
> and all the women went out after her in dance with
> timbrels. And Miriam chanted for them...."
>
> —Exodus 15:20

for Carol Kestler

we sing
as Miriam did
Miriam singer dancer
Miriam coper
Miriam who organized, managed, provided
who kept life's necessities in order
while her brothers
invented priestly rites
meditated on mountaintops
found God in isolation

Miriam who kept life's necessities in order
in order that her brothers
could
she sang

Miriam did you ever need your own
thicket
your own
pine forest
the privacy of giant granite boulders
five thousand meters away from the
hungry
Israelites

Miriam did you ever find your own
cloud enshrouded space?

Miriam
did you ever find your own

song?

MIRIAM THE PROPHET SPEAKS TO MOSES

when we came to the sea
I got my language back
gave it back to you

and the sea washed away
the strange syllables
of Pharoah's sentences

our language
will grow in the desert
but my words will encrust

like the scales on my skin
until your prayers
make the excess fall away

we danced
with the salt drying
on the hems of our skirts,

the smell of seaweed in our hair
but I want our drums and finger-cymbals
to coin new syllables of freedom

for that season,
which will come,
when I can no longer dance

THE BOOK OF LEAH

Genesis 29-35

A MIDRASH ON LEAH, NO. 1

Nowadays your father couldn't play his trick,
disguise your awkward body with a veil,
send you to your sister's wedding bed,

then give your husband your pretty sister, too.
Your modern husband chose you by himself
during the time you were thin, or because

that year he liked the poems that you wrote,
or because, after a night in a dark bar (the modern veil)
he got you pregnant. But when the novelty wears off

or passion goes the way of dirty dishes,
while you're in the kitchen saucing his favorite *pasta al dente*, or in
the library finishing your dissertation

he'll go back to your slender sister Rachel.
Even today, he'll have her too.

A MIDRASH ON LEAH, NO. 2

Leah, all my life
you have been hiding
out there in the desert,
behind the adobe walls
of your father's house,
hiding in the courtyard
of your husband's house,
hiding because your emotional eyes
could see what men thought they wanted

and it was not you.
Leah, you knew you were not chosen,
that only your father's games
brought your husband to you,
and that he did not want you,
it was your sister he wanted—
Rachel, shapely, beautiful Rachel.
And you'd heard what people said of you:
"She has a pretty face."

Leah, when they buried you
in the family cave at Machpelah,
they must have known how often we,
your dark-eyed daughters,
would need to call to you. Leah, Mother,
give us your patience,
the way to be brave, unjealous.
Show us the way to love when our husbands turn
to the shapely ones, the women
in the fashion magazines, their secretaries,
nurses, the colleagues in the English Department,
when they turn to our sisters. Leah,

walk with me to the well. Leah,
I will greet you, I will kiss you. Leah,
I will stay with you
even on the nights

when Jacob has left you alone.

LEAH TELLS RACHEL SHE WANTS TO LEARN NOT TO LET JACOB MATTER...

Remember the hill where we played near our father's home?
When we were girls we would take the sheep there
and talk—I talked, you laughed.

An acacia tree
clung to a wedge
of rock.

We could see the desert stretch south toward Bethel
like a clean blanket
that might have room for us both.

WHAT LEAH DID

Even when the children were young
I read a lot. And listened
to the stories the other mothers
told on the playground.

I became a weaver, and planted
a garden: dye-plants, madder
and henna.

Then I began
to walk in the mountains
searching for pot herbs:
hyssop, mustard, chicory,
rocket. I'd sit a long time,
watching for antelope.
Sometimes my husband's brother Esau
visits.

MEDITATIONS ON THE JEWISH YEAR

COMFORT

> Rabbi Isaac further said: Four things cancel the doom of man, namely, charity, supplication, change of name, and change of conduct.
>
> —*Talmud, Rosh Hashanah* 16b

When she was six years old
her sister took her to the American school
where the teacher asked her name.
Her sister told the teacher,
"Nechamah Leah" and the teacher said,
"Emma," so she named herself
"Emalene." From that moment

she created herself, an original woman.
Third daughter of immigrants, she
went to college, taught, became
a businesswoman, sold women's dresses

to schoolteachers, raised
three children, was proud of
eleven grandchildren. Instead of Comfort,

Emalene created action, turned a profit, yelled at her husband,
told stories. At ninety-five
the Angel of Death came looking for her
in a sixth-floor hospital room
with a window overlooking her schoolyard.
"Nechamah...Nechamah..." he called

but Emalene
didn't recognize the name, couldn't answer
to promises of Comfort,
lay in pain for weeks, fingers and toes
turning black for lack of blood,
averting the doom of man
until (the day before Rosh Hashanah)

she could no longer forget her name

EREV ROSH HASHANAH 5754, AT THE FOOT OF THE MOUNTAIN OF THE DESERT BIGHORN

for Imra Ben-Ami
below Pusch Ridge, Catalina Mountains, Tucson
Erev Rosh Hashanah 5754
15 September 1993

The mountains come closer at sunset.
The ram
Tekiah Tekiah
turns to face us on its purple cliff.
Tekiah. The ram
caught in the thicket,
given instead
of Isaac.
So it is the ram we see now
when we are called to its mountain by the *shofar*
to hear the disturbing story
we will puzzle over, if we dare,
attempting to create some *midrash*
that will peel our minds like a pomegranate skin
exposing the six hundred and thirteen *mitzvot,*
that will locate something stronger than our fears
that have allowed us to almost sacrifice
our sons, our daughters,
that have allowed us to send them away.
Red unripe seeds of pomegranate,
red blood, what have we done this year
to stop the blood? *Tekiah*

L'shana tova tikatevu...

Our lives are inscribed
in the unpolished furrows
and along the polished ridges
of the curving horn,
our lives have made as many turns
as the *shofar*
but what sounds will come out

in the end
Tekiah Teruah
loud enough to reach
God's ears?
The seeds of the pomegranate
scatter easily. The fruit
bursts open on the tree,
birds peck at the translucent red beads,
the cycle of drought and rain
splits the skin and rots
the seeds. *Mitzvot* so easily lost.
What can we gather here,
together?

Tekiah
Arafat reaching for the hand of
Yitzhak Rabin
while we remember someone who reached
for the hand of Isaac—
who was, in fact, 37 years old,
and not a helpless child
when he allowed himself to be bound
and needed a hand to reach for him
to stop the blood.

Tekiah Teruah
What can we gather here,
together? *Yom Hazichronot.*
Remember the good we have done
to turn pain into mystery.
To hold the hand of a depressed friend
and refuse to let go
To remember the blood and to refuse.
Tekiah.
Tekiah Gedolah.
Tekiah Shevarim. Teruah.
Tekiah.

NOTES:

Shofar is a ram's horn used as a ritual trumpet during Rosh Hashanah and Yom Kippur, the Jewish New Year and Day of Atonement. In ancient times the *shofar* served as a general instrument to call the population to attention for religious or political functions. *Shofarim* are often made from the intricately curved horns of Israeli desert sheep. In Tucson, Pusch Ridge is a mountain area which is the last stronghold of the increasingly rare desert bighorn sheep, which are threatened by encroaching development.

Tekiah, Tekiah Gedolah, Shevarim, and *Teruah* are instructions given to direct the rhythm and type of sound made while blowing the *shofar.*

Midrash: in Jewish literature, a story created by enlarging on a Biblical story or imagining what the characters in the story might do in somewhat different circumstances, thus enabling the writer to freely explore the spiritual significance of the original text.

L'shana tova tikatevu is the traditional Rosh Hashanah greeting. It means "May you be inscribed for a good year." According to tradition, God inscribes the names of those who will live during the next year in a book which is opened on Rosh Hashanah and sealed closed ten days later, on Yom Kippur.

The six hundred thirteen mitzvot: traditionally, there are supposed to be 613 commandments given in the Torah (the first five books of the Bible), which include both ritual obligations and ethical acts to be carried out. The pomegranate, packed with seeds, is said to contain that many seeds and thereby represents the Torah.

Arafat reaching for the hand of Yitzhak Rabin, after the signing of the Israel/PLO agreement in Washington, September 13, 1993.

Yom Hazichronot means "Day of Remembering," one of the traditional names for Rosh Hashanah, referring to our obligation (and God's) to remember how we have acted during the last year as well as to remember historical acts of righteousness.

YEDID NEFESH FOR EREV ROSH HASHANAH ON SHABBAT

    after the traditional hymn by R. Eleazar Azikri (16th century S'fad Kabbalist)

    —*Mahzor Hadash*, p. 8

Beloved of my soul, Father full of mercy,
hold me as You did when I was born.
You are the one my soul craves,
the residue of nectar on my lips.

Full of radiance, Your light would heal me,
bring me happiness forever. I come as your servant,
asking You to lead me, let me follow close along Your path.
Capture my passion in Your splendor. Let us dance:

A stately waltz, I bow to You.
A tango, full of drama and doubt.
A get-down blues, let me pour out my pain
against Your strong beat.
A slow dance, my head against your chest,
Your arms around my waist,

The way we used to.

Yedid Nefesh: beloved of the soul (Hebrew); a medieval *piyut* (poem) traditionally sung on the Sabbath, and sometimes sung on Rosh Hashanah when it falls on the Sabbath.

STAINED GLASS

Neilah, for my father

Then the sun slipped
bands of violet, bands of cyan
through the windows,
the colors lengthened
across the pews,
tinted the dry voices
of pages turned in prayerbooks,
colored the shuffle of mourners
shifting slowly from one foot to the other,
and color poured over their words,
spoke the Aramaic syllables for them,
gold exposed in a dry riverbed,

even at the end of the day,
darkness drifting into light.

Note: *Neilah* is the final service of Yom Kippur. In the Reform liturgy, it is immediately preceded by the *Yizkor* memorial service.

WE ARE AS A PASSING SHADOW, BUT YOU ARE ETERNAL.

—Mahzor Hadash, p. 461

My father dropped dead on the street
after he bought my cousin a Bar Mitzvah present.
My grandmother battled a barracuda
as she lay in her last hospital bed,
the hole in her heart refusing to give up.
My grandfather spoke to me from his heart
maybe for the first time,
and a week later he was gone.
My mother can't remember who she is.
I limp
I am short of breath
I am exhausted.
You are eternal.
Aunt Sarah and Aunt Ida stood next to me one Shabbat
Two Litvak daughters who were taught Torah.
Who will I stand beside?

Note: literally "You are eternal" is "*v'Atah Hu ushnoteicha lo yitmo*"—"You are the One ...Who does not die." This line follows the hymn *"Ki Anu Amecha,"* "We Are Your People" and is part of the Yom Kippur confessional service.

MI SHEBEIRACH I

    at the Cleveland Clinic

I stood by the open laundry room window
looking west
to the Plain Dealer tower
the Lake
the lights of Jacobs' Field
the flashes of lightning behind clouds
the darkness of the sky

The washing machine churned rhythmically
I saw the monitored graph of your heartbeat
the clothes slammed against the steel tub
I was as alone as the slamming of sex
I began to sing a *Mi shebeirach* to gather power
I sang to call your heartbeat out of your chest
to call your heartbeat to a regular rhythm

to bring all the strength that the mothers can bring us
and the power of fathers
Outside the window rain had begun to fall
heavy sheets of summer rain, with lightning behind clouds
The renewal of body
The renewal of spirit
my tears began to fall
alone in the laundry room
alone with the love of clothes churning against the steel tub
alone the only place I could call out this power to your heart

Thanks to Debbie Friedman, "Mi Shebeirach"

MI SHEBEIRACH II

I want to command the power of our ancestors to my mother's healing. All the ancestors—and her own husband, my father—who could not have valve replacement and bypass surgery, who died of heart attacks and congestive heart failure and strokes. All the ancestors who had children they judged and didn't understand, who loved them anyway. All the ancestors who were the children who loved their parents and wanted them to stay alive because perhaps there would be a reconciliation, or perhaps an opportunity to be successful enough to see more of each other. *Joseph and Jacob.*

Mi Shebeirach. With these words I command the power of our ancestors to my mother's healing.

LION OF JUDAH

Every year we put the white sock
on the rolling pin,
dusted it with flour,
rolled out the balls of white dough,
dipped the plastic shapes in flour,
and cut out dreidels, Stars of David,
candles, a wine carafe
and the Lion of Judah.
We carefully pressed the blue plastic hands and feet
head and curly tail
into the dough, hoping
it would lift in one piece and hold
till it fell gently to the cookie sheet.
Often the tail feel off,
or the foot disconnected itself
from the front leg. With a little water
we'd perform the necessary surgery.
"Rampant lion" they call this pose.
Lion of Judah, symbol
of the Maccabees. Lion serving God.
The gilt ones at the San Xavier Mission
were stolen one year;
they had to be replaced, the thief never caught.
The plastic edges wore down
on my mother's cookie cutters
but one year I drilled holes and turned them all into
a mobile I hang each year at Chanukah.
When my sister told a reporter about
the Lion of Judah cookies
for a Chanukah story in the *Pittsburgh Post-Gazette*
I cut down the Lion and pressed it carefully into dough,
trimming all around with a tiny knife, eight times, and
after icing them in royal gold and purple,
I shipped some to my sister and my mother as gifts.
Then I threaded the tiny bore with plastic line
and hung the mobile, its sky blue translucent Lion
hanging proudly,
once again.

SEASONS

    on Tu B'Shevat

At the Tu B'Shevat seder we drink four cups of wine
a cycle of white, pink, rose, red
to represent winter, early spring,
late spring, summer
to represent the state of trees

It's how I feel about you—
white, cold, hard
icy wine
and my body like a stiff leafless tree

A little red wine added to the second cup
Early spring
Blossoms of almonds, peaches
Light pink, white dappling the branches
allowing a little blood to color my cheeks.

The third cup mostly red, but mixed
with a little white—
it looks almost like red, but lacks the strong taste
of Merlot or Cabernet.
The leaves of the trees are opening
light green and narrow
The late peach, the plum trees are blossoming,
the heavy fragrance of the lime tree.
My arms encircle your waist.

The fourth cup, full red,
a promise of summer,
trees covered in full dark green
bearing peaches, apples, purple plums,
a rich kaleidoscope of sweetness
embracing you again.

Rosh Hashanah L'Ilanot
I will make this a new beginning

toward the full heat of summer
a promise
my fingers reaching out to touch your heart.

Rosh Hashanah L'Ilanot: New Year of the Trees, observed on *Tu B'Shevat*, the 15th of the month of Shevat on the Jewish calendar.

SEDER

The "Paschal Yam" sits on the tray
instead of a shankbone
              (although my mother served sweet potatoes
                  in orange cups
      every year).

At sunset we gather
to celebrate freedom
drink four cups of wine
eat four kinds of *charoses*:

Moroccan date balls wrapped in romaine,
Yemenite, apricots and pistachios,
a pyramid of dates from Iran.
        (I still prefer
             the traditional apples, walnuts, raisins, wine).

Shleime the Patriarch, my uncle's father,
who led my childhood Seders
making magic with his strong voice
so I could stay awake till two in the morning
as we raced through "*Echad Mi Yodea,*"
still stands behind me,

but tonight we read, mostly, in English.
Joann and I sing "*Avadim Hayenu*"
and I sing the *Hallel*, mostly, alone,
but there's always the young child
to sing the Four Questions
while Aiyana signs them, her fingers
dancing to the beat

as we all move
again
from slavery to freedom
and each year there's someone
new at the table
to bring with us

across the Red Sea.

URCHATZ

As we wash our hands without a blessing
I will notice the guest who pours the water
I will notice my hands softened by warm water
I will remember that Moses was saved in water
I will remember that Miriam found pure water
I will remember that water itself is a blessing.

ARIZONA THE ANGEL

Instructing us
to bring flowers from our gardens
to decorate the *shul* for *Shavuot*

the Rabbi tells us that when God
gave the Torah on *Har Sinai*
the bare rock of that desert mountain

burst into bloom, covered with sweet flowers

as here in Arizona, in a spring when rain
and the warm sun have slyly conspired
the hillsides blaze with poppies
and walking among boulders
owls clover, marigolds and penstemon
appear out of the gravel geologists call
"pavement"

Arizona the angel that has made me understand
the images of my people's Book.

GUARDING THE SABBATH

Remember the Sabbath Day and keep it holy.

–Exodus 20:8

Guard the Sabbath Day and keep it holy.

–Deuteronomy 5:12

When I was growing up, a Friday night did not go by that we didn't observe *Shabbas*. There would be the smell of chicken roasting, or baking with a coating of matzah meal and paprika (my mother's Jewish Hungarian "fried" chicken), and the smell of onions frying with one chicken liver to make chopped liver. I'd help by setting the table with a smoothly ironed white brocade cloth, carefully folded napkins, our good china and the real silver engraved with the initial "S" that I'd take out of the carved mahogany box with the crimson velvet lining.

When my father came home, we'd all sit down at the table and light the candles, sing the blessing together. For some reason, my father would strike the wooden match on the sole of his shoe and hand it to my mother or me to light the candles, and in my mind the image of my father bending over to strike the match to the sole of his shoe is merged with his reciting *Kiddush*, and to this day, when I begin to chant the *Kiddush*, I see my father, bending over, performing the magical act that signals the beginning of *Shabbas*.

At least every other week, my mother would explain proudly that we light the candles, together, when we're all together and ready to begin the meal, and not necessarily at sundown, because her Hungarian aunt, the one who insisted on returning to her elegant life in Budapest and thereby was sent to Auschwitz, criticized Grandma for not lighting the *Shabbas* candles till she came home from work, and therefore Grandma stopped lighting *Shabbas* candles altogether. But we were Reform, so we could light them whenever we could, and so we were better, truer to Judaism, than

Grandma who no longer lit them at all. And so I learned that tradition doesn't rule over meaning, and observance doesn't decrease over time, but may actually increase. And I always felt sorry for Grandma, who didn't enjoy *Shabbas* dinner.

Then my father would lift his silver cup of wine and begin the *Kiddush*. He chanted the entire *Kiddush*, in melodic Hebrew that I've only recently learned to fully understand, and then he'd ask each of us at the table to name one good thing that had happened to us during the week just past. And indeed, every week, we each had much to be thankful for.

And then we'd bless the challah, and my mother would pass a tiny dish of chopped liver, and we'd each spread a spoonful on our slice of challah, and *Shabbas* would be underway.

EVEN A SINGLE PASSION LURKING IN THE HEART HAS THE POWER TO OBSCURE REASON.

I Ching, 43, Kuai/Break-through (Resoluteness)

FIVE DAUGHTERS OF THE GARMENT TRADE

    in memory of Uncle Moe's remnants

The one thing
we'd learned to do
was sew.

Muriel describes
the fitted suit
cut from Forstmann
wool, she can't remember
the name for the weave—
finer than flannel,
not called gabardine....
She remembers the trim,
the flared skirt,
the nipped waist
of her youth.

Minnie remembers
her sister
the professor
who baked challah,
rugelach for a crowd,
prepared feasts
for family reunions,
but finally called long distance
to ask how
to thread a needle.

I remember Uncle Meyer—
stockbroker turned tailor
in twenty-nine—
showing me how to hold
the needle, my finger
behind the eye,
to trim the thread
on an angle
to push it through

each time.

Yvette remembers
the remnants, too,
reconstructs a certain
flowered print, recalls
making dresses for dolls,
costumes for Purim,

and Esther, once the smallest girl,
tells how her mother
dismissed each scrap—
it'll make a dress
for Esther.

Our stories fly
like needles, pull
cards wrapped with lace,
eyelet, buttons
from heavy cartons
wrapping each of us
in the nine-and-a-half yard
leftovers
of our shirtwaists,
blouses, bedroom
curtains,
slipcovers, lives.

WHEN IT IS WARM ON A SEPTEMBER NIGHT

When it is warm on a September night
and you lie on your back on the grass
the stars smell like warm dust
and the weight of the universe surrounds you,
knowing the direction is toward December
you feel, nevertheless,
the luxury of August.

There is nothing to do but lie there
smelling grass vapors, pungent like soup,
but less steamy, and the olive trees,
blowing silver-sided, rich and faintly fruity,
and the sky itself, heavy
and filled with the aroma
of velvet pulled from an old trunk.

When you lie on your back, hands behind your head
or at your side, not moving either way,
and your breath falls back into your throat
and you pull the warm air into your lungs
your body is a brick that will not change shape
when the Big Dipper swings its scoop
across the sky.

THE ARTIST RETURNS TO HIS GARRET IN PARIS

In the end it is hard to tell what is left:
postcards of impossible stones,
the tastes of thin rivers,
a dead moth on the sheets.
The question of where to eat dinner.
(There are many cafes here, and also
the home of a generous aunt.)
Snow still melts on your naked back
and you have taken off your clothes.
There was a time
when you had what you wanted:
bones, and a measure of magic.
You used them to pay for experiences
you wonder if you understand.
When you sleep the pigeons stand guard
like gargoyles. In the end
it is hard to tell what is left.

PLANTING BY THE MOON

First quarter, moon in Cancer, good day to plant.
I set out tomatoes: Red Cherry, Rutgers for the cloudy days,
Golden Boy and Yellow Pear. I dig a trench for beans.
I watch the earthworms wriggle when I turn the spade
to set out eggplants. I broadcast chervil, tuck in basil,
find the space where summer can begin.

We learned the rhythm quickly, watching zucchini grow
among black volcanic rock
on a desert hillside.
I watched you weave the tendrils of a beanstalk through the fence.
I watched you smile as you pulled the weeds.
And then you left,
the rhythm changed.
Dry earth choked back the summer growth.
I made the winter planting
but forgot its harvest.

This year I'll have three gardens,
a 3/4 measure of my peace.
I sowed lettuce in September,
peas and turnips and chard.
In October I planted
to survive the frost, with roots
that would huddle
beneath a quilt of soil.
Now, March 15 past,
I plant the summer crops,
squeezing peppers and zinnias between tall snow peas,
squash next to ferny carrots.

I've learned to fill my garden
as I've filled my life,
with flowers and small tasks.
In the jungle of green
fruits hang, waiting to be picked.
The rhythm will begin again.

I can say all this on a bright day
with warm orange-blossom on the wind,
the moon in Cancer, first quarter,
good day to plant.

SOLO

I walked along the edge of the water,
alone because I wanted to be alone.
There were no sea shells on the sand.

There were two Mexican girls
wearing short pleated skirts,
wearing thick socks and dancing shoes,

and they walked along the beach
holding hands. At the fish market
the vendors laughed when I tried

to spend my last pesos on shrimp.
On the drive home
I ran over the heads of many lizards.

AFTER THE ACCIDENT

in memory of Anna Marie Miguel

We watch the horses stretching their necks
to reach the water beyond the mesquite trees.
Remember, you wanted to learn to raise horses,
to work near the smells of alfalfa and horsesweat

and now you're a woman who doesn't remember
the school where you studied the feeding of horses.
To help you I point to your name on a textbook,
a large scientific book about horses.

I'm teaching you multiplication, you've lost it.
I make you repeat, sing-song, the patterns,
repeat the tables, the sixes, the sevens.
You make them into rows of horses,

horses that can't remember mesquite trees.
They stretch their necks in the sun,
toward the water. And you move to count them,
the warm rows of horses.

THE HANDMADE DRESS

Outside the patio door
he leaned to kiss me
and reached
his hand behind the crisp pique
of the sundress I'd designed
myself—under the appliqué of turquoise
and purple balloons. It was my first time
and probably his, his hand flat
and silent against my skin.

For the first time in my life
I was beautiful.

FOR WILL AREHART

After reading the obituary
I phoned my son,
confirmed it was the man I thought,
a teacher at his school,
a man who'd helped my son
grow up. AIDS, my son told me,
and then we hung up the phone
each to go on
with our chores for the day,
mine, to weed the garden,
sitting on dirt, pulling
clumps of invaders away,
grateful for this chore
to comfort me,
but I wanted to name
each plant I pulled out
and I regretted, too, an inability
to leave the plot in wildness.

DINNER AND A MOVIE WITH SUSAN AT THE HISTORICAL LANDMARK

I went to Susan's, later we went to dinner.
Cold split pea soup—which was actually good—
a salad, a spinach quiche we had to send back uneaten
(except for two bites to prove how bad it really was)
and a few bites from the replacement fruit, a plate
of watermelon, honeydew and pineapple
and a bottle of champagne to wash it down.
The waitress, sending the cork across the room,
asked us what there was to celebrate. Ourselves?
Susan smiled, said she likes champagne.
She didn't like the movie, though.

FOREST FLOWER

First I saw her, the woman from Japan,
in silk that smelled like apple leaves.
Her hair wrapped her back like black
silk unfastened from the bottom of a loom
They had been slicing swordfish, soaking it all night
in the juice of lemons. Outside their room
vines dropped over a concrete cliff.

He turned to me: "She doesn't need commitment."
I saw a row of men and women
standing in a trench, footings for a building.
Their bodies would be bolts to anchor walls,
their faces, our mothers and fathers, and I should
scream at them, "Get up and run." Instead

I grab a vine and call her name
as I rappel: Forest Flower. They begin
to eat bleached swordfish. They feed
each other with their fingers and I call her name
as though it were my own. *Even a single passion
lurking in the heart has power to obscure*

the kimono you have folded on her chair. My cat,
reflected in the pool, turns to me and whispers
from below the water: "It's been more than a month."
She smoothes her fur. She doesn't need commitment.

TRAVELS

At the German border the men on the train
told her in broken English
their suitcases were full of eggs,
not to put hers on top.
The man she was with shrugged,
led her to the next car,
despite the *couchette* tickets
she'd taken the trouble to buy
and the late hour. In Copenhagen
he tucked her under a puffy featherbed
and left her for a blonde
with cropped hair and a slight accent.

Later, wandering on a Mexican street,
she thought of him,
thought of those suitcases, how silly
she was to have listened to the German men,
to have listened to any men at all
although she was still listening
to the blond man who was walking
beside her that night,
listening to him talk
about fishing, about
the *huachinango* they'd just eaten,
about catching sailfish from a large boat,
about bargaining
with the supposedly illiterate *pescadores*.

It would only be later, when
he left her for a blonde
with long hair and no accent
at all, that she'd remember
the eggs, the suitcases, the fish
and both men, as well as others
who'd left her, or not,
and realize

that what she liked most
was to travel, to ride on trains
where the sound of the rails mixed
with several languages
she never understood.

THAT NIGHT

We went up to the bar
and ordered
a bottle of wine
and some clams
and the clams came
and you asked the waiter
for bread
to fatten me up
you said
and the wine was damn good
and so were the clams
all baked in wine
and bacon
and the sauce so good
soaked into the bread
and you saw they had
a bottle of *grappa*
and you told me
you'd make me drink some
some day
if you were mad at me
and the bartender
poured me a shot
and I drank it
and you promised me
you weren't mad at me
and never would be
and I liked the damn stuff
and went back to the clams
and the wine
and my arm
around your shoulder
and kissing you
and laughing and being drunk
together
and holding hands
and laughing
and sipping what was left of our wine

and the sauce from the clams
and the bread and the crumbs
and the red mountains and the drizzling rain
and knowing
how much we loved each other
that night.

THIN WALLS

In the next room a teacher chants
in loud, rhythmic Spanish
just below the level I can hear.
He must be conjugating verbs
or reviewing numbers.
Is it distracting my students,
silently writing their English exam?
Suddenly his room quiets as well
a low murmur in Spanish and English
as students, perhaps, clarify
what they are to do next. A laugh,
a higher woman's voice
come through the wall.
Are there days we talk so loudly here?
Vamos a ver
Por favor
OK, do it en español.

BLUE WILLOW

    for Joe

so we celebrate your birthday
with breakfast at Blue Willow
where you can order your favorite:
eggs, ham, potatoes,
extra slices of raisin toast,
coffee, orange juice

all the treats you'd cook for me
when you first moved in

I look up from my waffle
and catch your eyes watching
my face
so I look down
before you can see me smile

after seventeen years
you want everything casual
pretend to care
only a little

the maple syrup on my waffle
sweet
the salsa on your eggs
hot

THE COLOR OF THE MOON

The first melon of my harvest,
broken from the vine
small, pointed at one end.
I cut it open, a test
hoping that somehow it will have ripened
enough to eat. The flesh
is the color of the moon
dotted with sharp white seeds.
I cut off a chunk to taste
it isn't bitter
the flesh is not hard
I hold the chunk on my tongue
hoping for a sweet taste to melt out
and make me cut another bite
but nothing happens
there is no reason to eat this
I wonder
if I were starving
would this be of any use
and I must admit, no.
I leave the quartered melon on the counter:
Pale white, thin slice of green, cold white.

WATER AND EARTH AND HEAVEN, FISH WOMAN BIRD

     after a papercut by Tsirl Waletzky

Mayim
    ha-eretz
        Shamayim

Dancing Woman stands on the back of the smiling fish
her skirt, sash, *tallit*, earrings, hair
fly in the wind
she holds her tambourine to the sky
the caged bird inside stretches its wings to fly
opens its mouth to sing

Mayim
    ha-eretz (ha-ishah)
        Shamayim

earth turns water into heaven
under the bluest sky I place seeds into the soil
fragrant with the essence of fish
I place the seeds of American squash and corn
seeds of lettuce, onions, the garlic
of *Mitzraim*
call up the water *mayim*
from the earth
and down
from the sky

Mayim
    ha-eretz
        Shamayim

dam kacjim
heaven
and also *kacj* means ocean
the spread-out expanse
of water and sky

is the same in your language
as in mine

The entire universe is in my garden
each emerging seedling a poem
here, kneeling in earth
is my dance, the tender tips of red-fringed leaves
my song

Mayim
        ha-eretz
                Shamayim

this is what makes me woman
is the bird leaving its cage to sing
or visiting

shamayim
        ha-eretz

from heaven to earth
in my garden: cardinal
grackel sparrow quail dove
cactus wren hummingbird

u'uwhig:
sipuk
kakaichu, hohhoi
hokkad, wipsimal

malachim—angels
the messengers from heaven

language the connector
these are the same words

ha-eretz
ha-ishah
joins heaven and earth
separates them

and joins them back

ANTONIO'S NIGHT

I whisper
"*yo soy marrano*"
because I think
I recognize you.

You remember the word
from your history books,
secret Jews of the Spanish
Inquisition, but you didn't know

some had come to America.
There's not much
I need to explain.

In the illustration
Don Carvajal's sister Isabel
stands barebreasted

before the table of
Inquisitors. She is so young
in her boyish undershorts,
but her firm, full breasts

refuse to be embarrassed. Later
they will stand her on a cord of wood,
she will whisper "Shema" over the flames.

All night, we slap mosquitos
from each other's backs. When I whisper
"*te quiero*," you hear
"*soy marrano*," so we make love

as though we've known each other
four hundred years. If I did not tell you
who we are, this would be another
one-night stand. But we have recognized

each other. *Nuestro gente*. Before dawn

I'll wish that I could make you pregnant,
make you give me a daughter
who could teach me how to kindle *Shabbat*

back in New Mexico,
where I pick peaches
and raise pigs.

(reference is from Rochlin, *Pioneer Jews*.)

PITTSBURGH DREAM

(a meditation while swimming the half-mile)

At the Point the Monongahela is a quarter mile wide.
Below the bridge a dozen swimmers stroke

gray bodies through gray water, cross and back
as though no undertow could drag them downward

or downstream to Dravo's island, gray smokestacks
where Indians once grew corn, as though

no barges ever carried coal or sand
upriver to the mills at Homestead

where Uncle Moe would swim across
despite his mother's warnings

and I swim backstroke below flags
stitched zig-zagged to a wire floating west,

the direction the Ohio flows, alternating
red and white like the striped suit

you slipped off my shoulders one night and the world
hasn't been the same since. I never swam

the Monongahela but once I did swim far upstream
in the Allegheny, where it's clean

and willows sweep the banks
and even there I worried, worried

about the undertow and all the sinkholes
I'd been warned about. Why

did I drive across the Fort Pitt Bridge with you
last night, as though we were driving from our offices

to the house where I grew up? The whole time
I wanted to join the dozen swimmers in the river,

stroking hard clean freestyle straight across
as though the river had no current, straight as in the lanes

here in this pool, straight as the day
in the Gulf of California

when there was no wind and no surf and at high tide
half a mile was too far for you to see me

but I watched you and swam straight back to shore,
swimming toward you as though I knew what I wanted,

and our car crossed the bridge
and rode on through the Tubes.

TWICE NOW I HAVE THOUGHT

Twice now I have thought
I might not see you again. Once,
when the call came from Emergency
and again tonight, in my dream.
We were going off to become
a priest and a nun, but someone caught us
smiling at each other,
clasping our hands together tightly,
and threatened that if we didn't stop
we'd never see each other again.

Each time I caught myself,
had been trying to let go, to see myself
without you. We've chosen parts in different movies,
but the casting director wants to make
last minute changes.

I held your hand tight
so you wouldn't shake
while the doctor sewed your bleeding forehead
and I breathed every hope I'd ever had for us
into your palm, and dared to rest my other hand
against your thigh, not caring who
was watching. If this is love,
it won't be secret. But no one would pick us
out of a crowd, and we counted on that,
moving with the group like refugees.

You hand me a slice
of breakfast toast
like an offer of communion
but I have already picked up
the next script.

NIGHT OUT

>for Joyce

In French films it's always raining
and some Lucie or Nicole
wears a certain khaki parka
like the ones we wore in college.
So I ask for an umbrella
from the ancient *Book of Changes*
which offers me a woman
who waits three years to have a child.
In the end, the book continues,
there is nothing that can hinder.

In French films it's always raining
so I gather up my notebooks
and I walk out in the drizzle
to the nearest Chinese restaurant.
With my ticket stubs beside me
I should order something spicy
but I wanted the director
to walk me to the garden

to drink Beaujolais together
resting on his khaki raincoat
underneath a black umbrella.
In French films it's always raining
and the women never mind it.
The director follows smoothly
past the Oriental billboards

while the waiter brings my rice bowl
and I open up my notebooks
which are simply my umbrellas
and my own design for waiting
but it's only a night out
and the film is never over.

In French films it's always raining
but the children always dress well,
they wear velvet on the playgrounds,
they explore abandoned vineyards.
They ignore their parents' quarrels
like the waiter who ignores me

as I scribble in a language
he hasn't learned to read well.
When I ask for an umbrella
he replies it isn't raining.

FLOOD IN THE DESERT

The water did come up
above your waist,
the arroyo in flood, water rushing,
pulling you with it, bicycles
churning in a lake, tideless waves
covering your front steps.
Sooner than you might think,
ridges of sand, a beach at low tide,
pools of water in the stony places,
the frogs washed away
like the quart Bud bottles
piled against the fence, everything
swept clean. The neighbors stand
laughing on their porches, no one
comes home to see any of this.
Your lost dog floated downstream,
forced you to go for a walk, forced you
to notice its bones.
We are forced to speak
a language
neither of us knows and so
we build up clouds
every afternoon.

FARM REPORT, JUNE 2001

    for Erica

A few tomatoes are ripe
and I've shaded the rest, hoping
they'll make it through the heat.
There's lots of chard
and I'm cooking with it every night:
stuffed potatoes, pasta,
spanokopeta
and the other night, thin slices of red onion
for gardenburgers on homemade buns.
I've had one pepper, and more chiles
will be ready soon. I'll let you know
what we do with them, and when the eggplants
are ripe. Flowers
are more of a problem this year. The snaps are done
and the marigolds seem to have dried up.
The zinnias and sunflowers never got started—
I think the birds got them. The squash
have flowers but, so far, no fruit.
I think how you'll remember me for all the farm reports
I've sent since college, although
we've had plenty to say to each other all these years.
We send each other books, read them, and smile.
But when I tell you what really matters
it's in the farm report.

ON LISTENING TO A MOZART *ANDANTE*

Sinfonia Concertante for violin, viola and orchestra, K. 364

The *andante* asks questions,
considers grief
with questions slowly asked,
the weight of the answer too much.
And yet
the movement that follows
is *presto*,
the answer to grief
energy, how we can dance
our work again
in a festival of details
and grace, turning, turning,
returning.

MORNING PRAYERS ON THE PATIO, TUCSON

Bougainvillea the color of one morning
in Duke Sine's poster
of the Apache creation. Cracks
grow in the pavement
below the weathered blue doorway.
It's the morning after Seder.
All the guests have gone home.
It's warm already.
Fallen blossoms litter the brick
beneath the *etrog* tree
"Seek peace and pursue it."
My father's voice echoes
as I pace
as I pray

THE COLANDER

for Steve Carlat

The hands that made this bowl
set up a space for oranges
for pears for
peppers

left a luster to hide
behind figs
on a summer afternoon

the dancers in the glaze
under imaginary apples
escape through the drain-holes
and other silver clouds
float with cool green grapes
on a new-moon night.

TESHUVAH

    at the *Elat Chayyim* retreat center, August 1996

In my garden
Bermuda rhizomes
invade even oregano,
wax beans and yellow peppers
hide under meadows
of Johnson grass
past pulling.
Even ancestral paprika has been lost.

But here, at *Elat Chayyim—*
goddess of life—
Burgundy beans
shower from their leaf-laced fence.
Under dense red-veined chard
and straight stalks
fattening ears of corn
I search for
sprigs of plantain
leaves still close,
taproots thin,
dainty pigweed,
stray blades of grass
not yet embedded
in the clay.

Others before us
have cared for these beds
filled with cabbages
large as globes,
cosmos and zinnia suns.
Only my gardener's eyes
detect the weeds
and my leather-thickened fingers
grasp each one I find
pull it, toss it
to a bucket shared

with another weeder.
Joyful service they call it.
We speak Talmud as we work.

TEFILLIN

Wendy, May 22, 1996: I am sending you all of Grandpa Friedman's Prayer artifacts which I believe you will appreciate. I have had them for a few years now and have enjoyed taking them out and touching them, smelling them, looking at them.

If I unwrap the soft dark straps
If I place these cubes, carefully stitched,
which hold carefully scribed parchments
of ancient prescribed texts

If I place these objects on my arm,
my forehead, if I stand
within the defined space
and recite the Eighteen Benedictions

I will have to leap across a canyon
to the other side from which I know
I could not return

so I have left these Prayer artifacts, as she called them
in the soft brown velvet bag
every morning
I sit in the shade of an acacia
I face the growing, reddening globes of pomegranates
I feel the cool summer air on my arms

some of the words I say are old
some newer, more suited: I say
that I was made in God's image, not
that I am glad not to have been made
a woman, as Grandpa Friedman
must have been taught.

When did he use these tefillin?
The family legend placed his Bar Mitzvah
at the hospital bedside of his mother,
Ujhely, 1903

And afterward she died, and her daughter
was sent to Kolosvar
to a woman's education, the fine handsewn lingerie
of Hungarian aristocrats,
Auschwitz.
Nick lived in boarding houses with his widowed father,
refused to kiss the hands of the Romanian nuns,
was treated the greenhorn in American schools,
played gigolo on the ships—
when would he have *layn tefillin*?

Women are exempt from the time-bound mitzvot.
Women were not taught, forbidden,
unable, unwilling, unbothered...

It began with the photographs:
Great Grandfather Isaac, classic rabbi in stiff-band skullcap,
white beard, those piercing eyes
R. Yitzhak

then the prolific copies of the next generation
my sister's frequent darkroom gifts:
Lily, Lou and Ida
the Siegels: Gedalia, now George
(who went every day to Poale Zedeck—
I went with him till I was too old to sit by him
in the front row)
his wife Esther, the girls: Blanche, Fannie, my grandmother Em,
little Mo on Esther's lap...
My father and his brother Nate on an East Liberty street,
Harry Saul and Lily, probably their wedding portraits,
he with only a mustache, three piece suit, gold watchfob,
she in a high-necked Victorian shirtwaist, thin gold chain,
enigmatic smile on her face

I've already written about them
praying the way his father and grandfather
prayed in Lithuania, wrapping tefillin
on his arm while his wife
told not to interrupt

fixed breakfast for the homeless stranger...
Tzedakah trumps *tefillah*...

These are the faces when I recite the *Avot*
They are the reason I began to *daven Schachrit*
Then I found the line
that gave me the reason to go to my office each day
Blessed is God the King who loves justice and law.

If a woman can be frustrated in her work
If a woman can feel despair
If a woman needs to connect with her fathers

Will tefillin help? How will it change me?
How will I change it?

Some authorities note that women have sometimes used *tefillin,*
Rashi's daughters among them, and Saul's daughter Michal.

I have not been one to care whether women should or should not
    do something.
I have not been one to care for authority at all.

Why is this morning different from all other mornings?
On all other mornings you did what you wanted to do
(unless you had a pressing appointment with the Court)
Why on this morning have the literal words become significant?
On all other mornings you have felt no difference between men
and women.
Why on this morning are you so concerned that this is a practice
forbidden to women?
On all other mornings you do not wrap yourself even once?
Why on this morning are you considering wrapping twice:
one strap around your left arm,
the other to hold the box upon your forehead?
On all other mornings you have prayed without special ceremony.
Why on this morning are you making such a big deal out of it?

NO SENSE OF HISTORY

Palo Alto, California
July 20, 1969
Apollo XI
The First Men on the Moon

If you find letters I wrote
then throw them out.
I will buy a sketchbook
and colored pencils.

I will weave,
I will bake bread. One day
I will watch lunar dust

rise from the boots of slow kangaroos
on a TV screen
in California.
There are places I have never seen:

Dunlo, Berlin.
The things hardly mentioned out loud

will turn out to be true.
All the men
will be scholars.

CUTE LITTLE DARK BABY

    in honor of Arizona SB 1070

"What a cute little dark baby!"
My red-haired freckled mother's coworkers said when they saw
    me,
A darker skinned, dark brown haired infant.
"No," I said nicely to my third-grade friends who invited me to
play after school
In their houses in a "restricted neighborhood" where I knew
My family could not buy a house
And while there was no law that said I could not play there
I thought their parents would not like me to be there
With my dark skin and dark hair, just enough curl in it
To look Jewish, even though, apparently
My nose was not too long.
In fifth grade, dark skinned, long hair pulled back in a ponytail,
My classmates asked me
Are you Indian? (Meaning Native American, a name not yet
    thought of.)
Whose hand sewed the yellow star onto your coat? I thought
about my great-aunt
Who returned to Hungary from America in 1938
Wound up in Auschwitz but survived
And wrote letters to her brother, my grandpa,
Who read them to me.
People of color may not be safe

When I moved to Tucson everyone called me Anglo
And I looked around to see who they were talking about,
Me who had never been
Like everybody else.
And I knew better than to drive through the South
But in 1985
In Lafayette Louisiana
Joe and I were told not to go together
To a bar where a band we might like was playing
Because his skin is darker than mine
And he is Native American, and wears his long hair

Pulled back in a ponytail.
And I teach multicultural humanities at a college
Where all my students ask, "Why didn't we learn this in high
 school?"
And the State of Arizona has just passed a law
That high schools may not teach ethnic studies
And the State of Arizona has just passed a law
That anyone suspected of not having documents
Must produce them on the spot
Or be arrested
And deported.
And nobody asked Joe when they came to live on his land
And he hasn't called them illegal
But the State of Arizona might stop him
At their Border Patrol checkpoint
Because his skin is dark
And he wears his long hair
Pulled back in a ponytail
And he doesn't have a passport
And they might stop me
A cute little dark baby
Even though now my hair is gray
And they might stop you
But maybe not, if you have light skin and light hair
And never studied anyone else's culture
And don't speak anything but English
Because Arizona has just passed a law....

NOTHING TO DO WITH BEING OR FEELING JEWISH

> I told him how mad I was, to have piled on me jumping hurdles when I was so tired anyway. He regarded me with that cooling steadiness of his. When I was through, he walked to the window and I waited, miserable. Finally he turned to me again, and with a smile! "I'm quite certain that physical education is not essential in your case. I will excuse you from attending the course."
>
> After this things went better with me.
>
> —Anzia Yezierska, *Bread Givers*

Here I am, a middle-aged, overweight legal aid lawyer on the res, trying to fit into the sports-and-partying culture here (and have a little fun) by joining our office's SuperStars team, the Cholla Buds. SuperStars is a big deal here in Sells, with each separate office in town fielding a team for excessively serious events like flag football, relay races, sprints, egg tosses, free-throw basketball, a tug of war, and my chosen event, the hurdles.

My son's on his high school varsity cross-country and track teams, and I've been attending his meets since he was in 7th grade. Looked like fun, and no one else from the office was willing to try. (There's a rule that each team must have at least one member in each event.) So Kevin's been coaching me, helping me to imagine visualizing the hurdle before I get there, helping me to develop a rhythm for lifting my legs high enough and at an angle that will allow me to touch down and maintain momentum to run and jump the next one... I've never done anything this athletic in my life, although I once took fourth place in a swim meet (with only four contestants), and finally I learned to ski when I took private lessons from a lawyer from the public defender's office who took a leave of absence each winter to work at the slopes and treated me as a colleague, not a klutz.

Besides, most of the competitors are the local people who tend to be considerably overweight thanks to the effects of processed foods on bodies that evolved to survive on having food only half the year. If they can do it, I can do it. Of course, they've been playing basketball and volleyball and softball with their bodies since they were in grade school, and while I did the same thing when required for PE, I was scared of the ball and clumsy besides, so I was always the last one picked for any team.

But now it's time to take my turn. I've been practicing for a couple weeks, but only once with actual hurdles. I knocked most of them down, but I have managed not to break any bones. When the gun goes off, I start the race, instantly oblivious to my competitors. I'm only aware of my legs, doing something I've never let them do before. My right leg clears the first hurdle and my left leg follows behind, miraculously swinging over and landing ahead of my right foot, and I'm off, and I do it again, and again, and I let my swinging arms give me the momentum to fly through the air, like when I was a kid playing Peter Pan, but better, my legs feel longer than they've ever felt, I'm no longer 5'3, dumpy, slow, the last girl picked for the team...I'm turning into my own son, who's fast approaching 6'1", who runs and skis on long legs, who isn't here to see the results of his coaching...and as I clear the last hurdle and run to the finish line, I realize

I'll never do this again.

THE HUNGARIAN ART BOOKS

I discover two extraordinary volumes in my dream
one recent and surreal, contemporary art from Hungary,
the other a large book, filled with full-color plates
and dated nineteen fifty three: Hungarian art from that time,
hidden in a bookshop corner.

The older volume opens with a realistic still-life
of violins, but dark abstract-expressionist landscapes
dominate and lead me to recall
the stories my grandfather and mother told me
about our Hungarian relatives.
Uncle with a timber business in thick forests outside Budapest;
the land subdivided when the wood
ran out. A language where people say
their last names first. An expert now,

I am invited to speak
at a gathering of poets and artists
on the subject of Hungarian art. I begin
with the violins, recite my mother's stories, her grandfather
courting with a gypsy band. I conjure Bartok, the tense and
soaring String Quartets, the darkening and apprehensive Sixth.
And the dark streets, the crowded Communist apartments and a
            foreboding
of the tanks, and before that, Theresienstadt.

These books are thick and large
and printed on heavy, shiny stock. The others
help me turn the pages, one by one, and together
we discuss the meaning of each work,
knowing nothing of the artists.
The bookshop a narrow spine between houses,
medieval, hidden, full of treasure, filled with cerebral pleasures
and small-scale aesthetics. My Hungarian family

was elegant. Old photographs show them
in aristocratic dress, the women's hair piled in elegant buns,
the men wearing waistcoats and watch fobs,

in drawing rooms of polished wood, crushed velvet and cut
crystal. The women
wore hand-made underwear and served coffee and sacher torte
on tableclothes of delicate embroideries and lace. Who are these
        people
to whom I explain everything? Artists and poets, but they believe
I know what I'm talking about. Actually, I do,
though I haven't learned it in the usual way.
The man who invited me to speak puts his arm
around my shoulder, leads me into
the crowd. He looks like Will Inman. When I wake up
I'm still in the dream, can't open
my eyes. So I lie on the bed and try to join
the morning outside the window.
The dogs are barking at nothing,
the chickens make noise in response to the rooster,
and down the hall my family makes breakfast,
watches the news. I want an explanation
or a chance to rewind the film. I want to get up and put on
a Bartok record, but I don't, I wait until I realize

there's really nothing to explain. Then later that day
        a catalog arrives. A bargain book—*Hungarian Art: the*
        Twentieth Century Avant-Garde.
All here, except the violin. A painting of a carousel
        could be a violin. Forests, trees in a City Park,
trees behind and beneath
a seated woman's knees.
a 1937 untitled painting by Lajos Vajda (Vajda Lajos is how he
        would have signed it)
three houses in his village, the inside of a room, a manuscript
in English, German, Magyar, and in Hebrew script and print...
I cannot read them all...

Then Vajda's colleague Amos Imre, drawing dark houses and
horses and an angel/woman in the midst of war,
murdered in Germany,
nineteen forty four, and
sixteen years later his wife Anna Margrit
paints a shouting woman

with the tethered feet
of a bird.

GUILLERMO KAHLO

Guillermo Kahlo
a Hungarian Jew
a photographer
photographed old buildings in Mexico
moved to Mexico because he disliked the man
his mother married
grew up in Baden Baden Germany
but he was Hungarian.
About the Hungarian Jewish photographer Andre Friedman
known as Robert Capa
a friend was known to say
Hungarians are photographers, artists
because no one else can speak their language.
Capa photographed wars
Kahlo photographed old buildings
in Mexico that might as well have been
old buildings in Hungary
domes
stone
and he encouraged his daughter
the one we all know, Frida
gave her paints, an easel
gave her color, the bright reds and greens and yellows
let her paint his house blue,
let her know he was a Jew.

TALAVERA

This may be the tenth time I've chosen
These painted Mexican tiles
For countertops, backsplashes, windowsill.
This time I choose to make
A patchwork
Of blue birds flying
To the four directions,
Green birds trailing blue tailfeathers,
Four-colored geometries
Abstract green flowers
And bright squares of solid blue,
Yellow, green. I've done this
Again and again, covered
Surfaces in my own homes
And created gifts for others,
Choosing patterns myself
Or asking others
Which design they like.
The finished counter satisfies me,
I run my fingers over the shiny glaze
Against the thin path of gray grout,
Across the hard back of *pajaro azul*
Somewhere in this countertop
Descendent of Moorish *azulejos* in Toledo,
Mudejares and *conversos* in Puebla,
All the loves I've buried
Have returned, their yellow suns
Opening a way through the desert.

SNAKES

Our dog BB's head, blown up
from the snakebite

The dream
rainbow-colored snakes
twisted and curled
at the foot of my bed

The dream
he sent the snakes away

Snakes are my buddies, he said.
After that
I didn't want anyone else.

Hung a wooden snake
its body cut in segments
curled like a real one

above the bedroom window.
When he stopped
touching me I took it down.

The day a young rattler entered
the kitchen and a friend helped us
lift it on a long pitchfork
drop it over the fence into the desert
—Never kill a snake
They are part of life.

Snakes
when I read your story
all I thought about
was BB's swollen face
and the wooden snake
still curled in the drawer
where I keep

pillow cases.

DECEMBER 9, 1980

"Imagine" on the clock radio
woke me up
I lifted my head to look at the time
The next song was also John's
I said to myself
"He must have died."

I was lying on a thin foam mattress on the floor
I'd just left my husband
and it wasn't the week I had the kids
when they would have had this room
and I would have been in the living room
on the couch
I lay there and listened to the radio
"Eleanor Rigby" and "Norwegian Wood" both played
before the DJ said aloud
"John Lennon was shot last night
in front of his New York apartment"

It was a Tuesday morning.
I was supposed to be at work.
I lay there on the thin mattress
to the turns of "Double Fantasy"
waiting till they'd play "Imagine" again.

OVER A BEER

I sit across the table
last night from one man,
this afternoon another—
men I have loved
who have loved me
and now there is little to say
or there is much to say
but little reason to say it
I put a wedge of potato into my mouth
taste the tang of ketchup
remember when just watching him
had a bite
I sip my beer—
this is the best part—
the glasses are small
we've ordered a pitcher
he pours for me,
I pour for him
like we used to
We talk about a job
he's been offered
and turned down
no benefits
a waitress comes by
he introduces us
I wonder
if he's sleeping with her
The other man, today
grumbles about the limited selection of beer
I make complaints to him as well—
broken faucets, cracked tiles by the door
He takes what he can get—a Beck's
tells me about the job offers
his sons have gotten
I can't remember what his hand felt like
long ago on my back, my thigh
I pay no attention to his food

he pays no attention to mine—
though he insists on paying for it
Tired, tired
I sleep alone
There will be others
There will be others

L'EGLISE ST-ETIENNE

      France, 1966

At ten o'clock the sun hangs blue shadow tapestries
on the grey blocks at Caen. The choir sings
an Alleluia in Dorian mode, weaves bass and alto
through stone walls.

Beside red bird-of-paradise the bride and groom
kiss uncles and aunts
dressed in business suits
and slippery dresses. It is Friday morning.
The men have left their offices for this.
I would like to eat an orange,
to smell the peel on my fingers
all day long. The tour guide chants

*"C'etait construit par Guillaume le Conquerant,
l'annee mille soixante-six."* My husband asks me
what it means. The bride and groom
will go to live in their postwar apartment
with the yellow plastic kitchen
we've seen in Bauhaus magazines.

Along the river marigolds are blooming. Swans
turn their heads toward us. He puts his arm
across the bench. When I lean back he pulls his arm away
takes an orange from his pocket,
neatly severs the skin with his knife.

Our hotel overlooks this church. White lace
will veil the sun when we return
this afternoon, my body giving itself to him
as, *"la porte se donne sur la rue."* Below our balcony
soft blue festoons the street. On the dresser
orange peels, an empty wine carafe,
his tie. It is summer. We
have left our offices for this.

ALTER KACYZNE

after *Poyln: Jewish Life in the Old Country*

his name a replacement
for a dead older brother

wrote and photographed
Polish Jews but *The Forward*
wouldn't pay him
for both arts.

In 1925 his lens
captured three men
sitting on boxes
in front of a closed shop
in Tarnapol

next to the door
the wall is plastered
with posters
announcing
in Polish and Yiddish

"*Alter Kacyzne—a lecture
on Literature—A National
Treasure.*" These men
have no idea

Two of them converse
one, his cane across his knees
and the other
holding a book in his lap.
Each has a long, untrimmed
gray beard. The third man
rests his upright head
on his hand and looks,
under the brim of his hat,
at Kacyzne. This one's beard

is neatly trimmed, and only partly
gray. The caption of the photograph
points out that it is Sunday. By law
the stores are closed.
Next to the man
The roll-down door
sports a carved lock
and through the window
framed in rounded oak
we see a jar of pretzels
baskets stacked four high
dried fruits hanging on a string.

What does each man think?
Does the man who looks
know his photograph
will be published in America,
to remind those who've made it
where they came from,
what remains of old Poyln,
to urge them to send money,
tickets? Are the men who talk
oblivious of the camera
or were they posed? And is the man
behind the lens
thinking

of what he has to say
about Literature, or composing
a poem in his head,
or wondering
who he might have been
had his older brother
lived?

THE YOUNG WOMAN CONSIDERS THE UNTHINKABLE

At the edge of the forest
the black ice mocked her
Go back, back to your village,
the shtetl, back
to your own place.
Back to the safe lights
of *Shabbas* candles

but she lifted the plaid shawl from her shoulders
and waved it like a flag in the cold air
and soon
only the reflected birch
waved back.

ASTHMA, JUNE 6, 2000

After 3 I make it to Eegees for lunch
and a moment alone
but there are ten kids in Wildcat t-shirts ordering
5 different flavors of slush drinks
and more combinations of sandwiches
and one kid—not the look I would have picked—
reminds the cashier he hasn't gotten
his ranch dressing on the side
finally I'm waited on but this time
the cashier forgets the $5 bill
that should have been my change
when I sit down and open my sandwich
hot veggie grinder on whole wheat
oozing mozzarella, tangy chunks of tomato
and carrot, black olive slices and
a pepperoncini I might even eat
I realize I can't breathe, I'd forgotten
the doses of inhalers and pills
that were due at noon
with a spoonful of lime slush
the drink-of-the-month
I swallow a capsule of theophylline
take a shallow breath
and pull out David Lehman's new book
of poems, *The Daily Mirror.*
A mailman's sitting in a corner booth
reading the paper, wiping his mouth,
his mail truck parked outside the window.
The hot pepper is too much for me
Now the kids have all left
it's quiet and I'm up to "June 6th."

TOMATOES

Tomatoes wait in a white bowl
on a white linen cloth she found
at Yesterday and Today, and a bunch of basil
waits in a wooden bowl, waits
for the cook to chop it,
and a basket lined with a blue napkin
holds a loaf of crusty French bread.

The customers won't be here till six.
She uses the table for an easel,
paints still lifes with vegetables,
pours Beaujolais just to balance the glass.
It's not a model, no experiment.
There will never be a canvas.

Afternoon light bends Mingus on the stereo.
The flowers on the windowsill aren't right,
anemones turned too far to the side.
She painted the wooden chairs pink, light yellow,
an aqua paler than pastel. The backs don't match.

Will the paper sent a restaurant critic
or an artist? She doesn't want her life reviewed,
even on page 12. The customers will be
intruders, they will have their expectations
and opinions.

NOVEMBER 22, 1963

I was on a bus rolling through Connecticut
to meet my boyfriend in New York
We'd made big plans: he'd have a hotel room
thanks to his college marching band
and we'd spend the whole night together
for the first time. My friend Marie

had come along for a blind date
with Steve's roommate. She
was from Indiana, looking forward
to the Empire State Building
and Times Square. Somewhere
south of New Haven

the driver stopped the bus. "On the radio,"
he said, turning to face us, "on the radio, they said
'The President's been shot.'"
Before the Triboro Bridge we knew
the President was dead. Marie asked me
what we'd do. "Meet the guys,"
I said. "But I don't think
they'll play the game."

We went to the band's hotel.
We met the guys.
The woodwind section was watching TV
in the lobby. Over and over
we stared at Jackie...
Steve and I slept together the whole night.
I don't remember the sex.
I don't remember what Marie did.
The next day there was no game.
We skated in circles
on the Rockefeller Center ice,
but what was the point?
Her contact lenses scratched her eyes
so Marie was blind for a week.

JFK was dead.
We had to grow up fast.

THE LAST NIGHT

The last night we were together he brought out
a framed photograph of a semi-circle of men
in white hoods, a gathering of the Fort Payne, Alabama Klan
circled in front of a curving fence of dark, peeled stakes.
In front of them, like a large black spot
another group of men bent over, on their knees,
praying or begging to be initiated.

He told me his mother's grandfather is there
though he can't identify which hooded face it is.
He told me he gave an antique dealer $900,
and as he touches my Jewish face
with his soft hand, I ask myself,
but cannot question him:
What is this photograph to you, and why
are you showing it to me?

IN JANUARY

Two bags of chicken feed wait
in the back of my truck,
too heavy to lift,
so the hens starve slowly,
scratching for insects in what's left of their straw.
There haven't been new eggs for weeks.

On the South Side of Pittsburgh old Polish houses
shingled with green asphalt siding
wait for the snow to melt from the stoops.
On the evening news here they ran a feature on *pierogis*,
long tables of toothless women in babushkas
crimping the dough. The phone rings too often.
Sometimes it's you

and when you ask me how I am I lie.
What else is there to do?
Even on the farm you follow me,
like the hens forcing innocent potato bugs
underground, the lucky ones. . . .

THE SICK GIRL

> "*Ismeretlen fényképészé Beteg kislány*, 1910"
> ("Unknown photographer, Sick Little Girl, 1910")
> photo postcard purchased at The Hungarian
> House of Photography, Budapest

Behind owl-framed glasses, her eyes open wide.
The sick little girl, propped up in bed on lace pillows,
rests her arms on a velvet pillow, red probably,
or dark blue, embroidered and tasseled
in gold. A book lies, closed, on top.
Her lips try to smile, but don't.
I think she would like to hear me read a story.
If she were stronger, she might read to me.
She's old enough to read, ten perhaps.
Towels are draped over the foot of her bed,
after her mother, who nurses her without pity,
washed her face. The light gathers
on the girl's left cheek, on her left shoulder and wrist,
behind a jar of flowers. Perhaps, when she gets up from her bed,
her mother will help her walk.
She looks directly at the photographer
who has brought his equipment to her bedside.
Perhaps he has been commissioned
because the prognosis is not good,
or perhaps, the unknown photographer
is her father or uncle, perhaps even her mother,
using the sick young girl
as a model. I look into her eyes, which also look toward me,
full of stories and secrets.
I want to get her out of bed.
Even now she is reading to me.

LACE CURTAINS

In each window of the houses
lace curtains hide the life inside
In shop windows
bolts of lace stand or lean
on display
and all tell stories
In Paris, ducks float
on a web of diamonds
In Prague, ships unfurl their sails
against rows of waves
In the windows of Ukrainian cottages
birds fly: sparrows, doves,
even storks,
but no hawks or eagles.
There are roses, daisies, tulips
marching across in softly folded rows
in the windows of Budapest
and in Hungarian villages
the towers of the famous Count's castle
on the hill behind the towns
loom over the Tisza, repeated
on each panel
while dense forests alternate
with salmon leaping
or the proud antlers of grazing deer.
All white, filigree, in the winter
they must hide behind draperies
of forest-green velvet
or ride against seas of dusky satins.
But in the July sun they sing,
a dazzling vision
and each room bathes
in the joyous sun.

KOSZI, KOSZI

The one word we've learned to say
is *"Koszonom,"* thank you,
and at every opportunity
we practice. Our hosts repeat it back,
in shorter form, *"Koszi, Koszi"*
with wide grins and dancing eyes
as they hand us our change
of small shiny coins, our packages
of paprika, our velvet vests,
the blue and white candlesticks
carefully wrapped in bubbled plastic.

"Koszi, Koszi" we say to the young boy,
excited to practice his English,
who shows us on the map
that my grandfather's house is too far down the road
to walk, we should take the bus.
The old woman who hangs out the window above us
confers with him, grins at his accomplishment
and at ours. *"Koszonom,"* we say to her,
and she smiles even wider, *"Koszi, Koszi."*

WAR/PEACE

AT A MIDDLE-EASTERN RESTAURANT

The owner's son plays junior high school soccer.
He lies on a table outside
and through the window watches me eat
the food of his father's childhood,
a vegetarian soup, peppery lentils,
such a thin yellow you'd hardly know
it's made of beans,
but full of mint and lemon,
and right now the owner is reaching his hand
into a gutted lamb that hangs on a meat hook
just inside the open kitchen door.
I turn my eyes back to my bowl.
I eat my soup. The soccer player
slides himself off the table
like a slippery fish on the dock.
It's just started to rain.
I keep on eating my soup.
There are lemon groves and fields of mint
where the owner's cousins and mine
may be murdering each other.
I keep on eating my soup.

DREAD, PEACE, AFTER RADNOTI

(Enny's House, VII Budapest, Verseny u. 20)

halott néném jutott e szembe s már repült
feletten mind, akit szerettem és nem él,
sötéten szállt seregnyi néma holt,
s egy árnyék dőlt el hirtelen a házfalon.
Csend lett, a délelőtt megállt.

I thought of my dead aunt and in a flash it seems
all the unliving I had loved were flying overhead,
with hosts of silent dead the sky as darkened then
and suddenly across the wall a shadow fell.
Silence. The morning world stood still.

—Radnóti Miklos, "*Béke, Boryalom*" ("Peace, Dread"), 1938

I think of my dead aunt and in a flash it seems
all the unliving I had never known, but love,
are flying overhead
with hosts of silent dead the sky brightens
and suddenly across the wall a shadow falls. Silence.
The morning world stands still.

With a train ticket from Buchenwald, she came back to this
      house,
"laced under guardianship," the year I was born.
I knew she existed, my grandfather's sister who wrote him letters
from an ashen world. I had no way to meet her.
I knew she had a son the Nazis murdered. I knew
about murder, followed the Rosenberg case
on our new TV.
              That's why I couldn't know her—
the Communists. My grandfather couldn't mail his sister
a package of stockings, a dress, some cash,
a photograph of me. He routed them through Canada,
through family there, their government less paranoid.
Impossible to visit.

Csokolom, I kiss your hand. Aunt Enny, I would have kissed
        your hand
if I'd been able. Instead, more than fifty years after
you sold this house, I track it down, find it
so close to Keleti Station, take photographs,
try to explain to the people who live there now.

I photograph the house, the courtyard, the garden. Your shadow
silent against the wall.
And the hosts of all the silent dead
whose names and numbers I have studied
brighten the sky. *Csokolom*, they whisper.
My morning world stands still.

HOW TO SURVIVE IN THE 21ST CENTURY

September 11, 2001

Learn how to run calmly.
Don't wear high heels.
Learn to pray in the ways of at least two religions.
Keep a cell phone with you at all times.
Tell your mother you love her.
Carry a dust mask.
Learn a language that only ten thousand other people speak.
Pray in the ways of the religion you like the best
but don't forget about the others.
Swallow your breakfast while watching people
jumping out of windows.
Tell your brother you love him.
Cultivate a garden. Plant swiss chard and sunflowers.
Breathe.
Don't wear high heels.
Tell your mother you love her.
Eat more rice.
Plant a lot of flowers.

A NOTE ABOUT LANGUAGE:

Many of the poems in this book include languages other than English: French, Spanish, Magyar, Hebrew, and Tohono O'Odham. This technique, known in literary criticism as "macaronic poetry" because one language is inserted into, and fills spaces in, the other, does not require knowledge of the second language. The reader should be able to appreciate the sound and just the idea of another language being included. Of course, for readers who do understand the additional language(s), additional depth will be evident.

Lynn Saul

is a poet and writer whose work has been published in a number of literary magazines and anthologies. She has also published several chapbooks of poetry, including *Family, I am Trying to Understand*, and *Nashim B'Midbar/Women in the Desert*. Her book about her exploration of her Hungarian Jewish family, *Learning to Say "Satoraljaujhely,"* was published by Jumping Cholla Press in 2010.

Lynn Saul earned an MFA in creative writing at the University of Arizona.

After a long career as an attorney, including eight years as a legal services lawyer on the Tohono O'Odham Nation in southern Arizona, Saul retired from the practice of law to focus exclusively on writing and teaching. She teaches writing and humanities at Pima Community College in Tucson, Arizona. She also leads community and synagogue writing workshops.

Joyce Septimus

is an artist living in Tucson, Arizona.

Cover art is adapted from her "Table Setting," acrylic, mixed media, and collage on canvas; 50" x 60"

www.ingramcontent.com/pod-product-compliance
Lightning Source LLC
Chambersburg PA
CBHW062206080426
42734CB00010B/1806